# Legacy of the Desert

# Legacy of the Desert

---

## Understanding the Arabs

### By Jules Archer

Little, Brown and Company · Boston · Toronto

FIRST EDITION

T 10/76

Library of Congress Cataloging in Publication Data

Archer, Jules.
  Legacy of the desert.

  Bibliography: p.
  Includes index.
  1. Arab countries—Politics and government. 2. Arabs. 3. Jewish-Arab relations—1917-
  I. Title.
DS62.8.A7  301.29'56  76-27757
ISBN 0-316-04965-4

Designed by D. Christine Benders

*Published simultaneously in Canada
by Little, Brown & Company (Canada) Limited*

PRINTED IN THE UNITED STATES OF AMERICA

For

**Kirsten Archer**

# Contents

| | | |
|---|---|---:|
| Table: How Nations of the Arab World Rank | | viii |
| Map | | x |
| Introduction | | xiii |
| 1 | Explosion in the Middle East | 1 |
| 2 | Through Arab Eyes | 10 |
| 3 | These Are the Arabs | 22 |
| 4 | Inside the Arab Family | 36 |
| 5 | The Days of Glory | 46 |
| 6 | Under Despotism and Colonialism | 61 |
| 7 | The Arabs and the Jews | 77 |
| 8 | Israel Is Born | 88 |
| 9 | Nasser Challenges the West | 98 |
| 10 | The Six-Day War | 115 |
| 11 | The Arabs Strike Back | 131 |
| 12 | The Helping Hand from Moscow | 148 |
| 13 | The Arab Superweapon—Oil | 155 |
| 14 | Black Gold and the Arab People | 168 |
| 15 | The World Looks at the Arabs | 179 |
| Bibliography and Suggested Reading | | 193 |
| Index | | 199 |

# HOW NATIONS O
## in size, populatio

| Size<br>(square miles) | Population |
|---|---|
| 1. Sudan (967,500) | 1. Egypt (37,000,000) |
| 2. Saudi Arabia (870,000) | 2. Sudan (16,000,000) |
| 3. Libya (679,400) | 3. Iraq (11,000,000) |
| 4. Egypt (386,000) | 4. Syria (6,000,000) |
| 5. Iraq (186,000) | 5. Yemen, Arab Repub. |
| 6. Oman (82,000) | (5,900,000) |
| 7. Yemen, People's Dem. Repub. (81,000) | 6. Saudi Arabia (5,300,000) |
| 8. Yemen, Arab Repub. (75,000) | 7. Lebanon (2,800,000) |
| 9. Syria (71,000) | 8. Jordan (2,400,000) |
| 10. Jordan (38,000) | 9. Libya (2,000,000) |
| 11. United Arab Emirates (33,000) | 10. Yemen, People's Dem. Rep. (1,225,000) |
| 12. Kuwait (6,000) | 11. Kuwait (1,000,000) |
| 13. Lebanon (4,000) | 12. Oman (600,000) |
| Bahrain (4,000) | 13. United Arab Emirates (230,000) |
| Qatar (4,000) | 14. Bahrain (200,000) |
| | 15. Qatar (100,000) |

*Excluding nations of the Mahgreb.

# HE ARAB WORLD RANK
## teracy, and gross product*

| *Literacy* | *Gross National Product* (per capita) |
|---|---|
| 1. Lebanon (70%) | 1. United Arab Emirates ($31,300) |
| 2. Jordan (55%) | 2. Qatar ($21,000) |
| 3. Bahrain (46%) | 3. Kuwait ($9,600) |
| 4. Syria (40%) | 4. Libya ($4,500) |
| 5. Egypt (26%) | 5. Saudi Arabia ($4,400) |
|     Iraq (26%) | 6. Bahrain ($1,750) |
| 7. Oman (20%) | 7. Oman ($1,500) |
| 8. Sudan (19%) | 8. Iraq ($1,000) |
| 9. Yemen, People's Dem. Rep. (15%) | 9. Lebanon ($656) |
| 10. Yemen, Arab Repub. (10%) | 10. Syria ($270) |
| | 11. Jordan ($261) |
| | 12. Egypt ($230) |
| | 13. Sudan ($120) |
| |     Yemen, People's Dem. Rep. ($120) |
| | 15. Yemen, Arab Rep. ($82) |

# Introduction

FOLLOWING the Six-Day War between Israel and the Arab Nations in 1967, a series of explosive events arising out of that crisis shocked and frightened the world.

An Arab cartel imposed an oil boycott on Western nations, causing oil prices to soar so high that even when the boycott ended, many countries were threatened with economic disaster. New clashes erupted in the Middle East, and the involvement of the United States and the Soviet Union on opposite sides led to fear of a possible nuclear holocaust. Desperate acts of political terrorism broke out in country after country, designed to compel attention to Arab grievances.

At the center of this Middle East cyclone was one basic conflict — violent opposition by the Arab nations to the Jewish state of Israel established in their midst by the Western nations in 1948. Displaced Palestinian Arabs had become homeless refugees, ignored and forgotten by the Western world. From their ranks came the Fedayeen commandos dedicated to regaining the Palestinians' homeland at any cost.

The security of the non-Arab world was shaken by their acts of terrorism, and by the Arab nations' persistent threats of war. In Western eyes the Arabs seemed a savage people, the Israelis defenders of civilization in the Middle East.

The Western world, familiar with the long and distinguished history of the Jewish people, had only sparse knowledge of the Arab contributions to human history and culture. We are not familiar with even one modern Moslem author, and the only Arab classics we know are the *Arabian Nights* and the *Rubaiyat*.

That there was more than one side to the Arab-Israeli conflict was suggested by Major General Carl von Horn, former chief of staff to the UN Truce Supervisory Organization in the Middle East. He found the Arabs "difficult, intolerant, indeed often impossible" to work with. But they were still more reasonable, he reported, than Israeli officers and officials who told him flatly, "You are either for us or against us," rejecting any impartial, objective approach to mediation.

We have good reason to try to understand the Arabs better. Our own well-being may depend upon it. Miscalculations in our dealings with them, as a result of our involvement in the Middle East conflict, could embroil us in another war far from our shores. The energy crisis we face, deeply affected by Arab decisions, also makes a better understanding imperative. The price and availability of oil affects our entire way of life — our industry, our transportation, our winter heat, our hot water, the food on our table.

This book was undertaken as a modest effort to make the Arabs more understandable to young Americans bewildered by Arab oil policies, Palestinian terrorism, and Arab-Israeli wars, since it is they who will influence our foreign policy in the Middle East tomorrow. In no sense special pleading, the book is neither pro-Arab nor anti-Arab; neither pro-Israel nor anti-Israel. I have tried to be as objective as possible.

Generalizations about Arabs must obviously be qualified by acknowledging many exceptions to the rule. Each Arab nation has its own unique folkways and characteristics. I have sought to focus, however, on those qualities and views which *most*

Arabs share, either through their common heritage in the brotherhood of Islam, or as a result of their suffering under four centuries of oppressive foreign rule.

I wish to express my gratitude for the generous help I received from Margaret Pennar of the Association of Arab-American University Graduates; Marwan Kanafani of the League of Arab States Information Center; Gazi Chidiac, Consul General of Lebanon in New York; the Jordan Mission to the United Nations; the Permanent Mission of Iraq to the United Nations; the Saudi Arabian Mission to the United Nations; Vladimir Belyakov of the Embassy of the Union of Soviet Socialist Republics; and the Union of American Hebrew Congregations. None of these sources is responsible for the interpretations expressed in this book, which reflect only my own views as the result of intensive research and of travels in Arab regions of North Africa.

Since the English spelling of Arabic names and terms varies considerably from translator to translator, I have chosen the spelling most commonly used in the American press.

Jules Archer

Pine Plains, N.Y.

# Legacy of the Desert

# 1

# Explosion in the Middle East

SEPTEMBER 1970. Four Western-owned jet airliners are skyjacked simultaneously by Arab commandos — the Fedayeen ("those ready to sacrifice themselves for a cause"). One Pan-Am 747 jumbo jet is forced to fly to Cairo. After it is emptied of passengers and crew, it is blown up. Three jets are forced down at an abandoned World War II fighter strip in northern Jordan, twenty miles from King Hussein's palace in Amman.

Defying Hussein, the Fedayeen terrorists proclaim the airdrome "liberated territory" under the jurisdiction of the Popular Front for the Liberation of Palestine (PFLP). They threaten to dynamite all three airliners with everyone inside if the Jordanian army makes any attempt to rescue the hostages.

World opinion is outraged. Why should innocent travelers

and flight crews unrelated to the Middle East conflict be kidnapped and used as pawns to compel European governments to free PFLP terrorists imprisoned for other skyjackings? Some embarrassed Arab governments, and other Fedayeen groups in the Palestine Liberation Organization (PLO), disavow the PFLP.

The terrorists release all passengers except fifty hostages. These are held until West Germany, Britain, and Switzerland agree to free seven PFLP prisoners. Then the three airliners are blown up on the Jordanian airstrip.

Furious at the PFLP's affront to his authority, King Hussein orders his army to attack all Palestinian commandos quartered in Jordan. Thousands of Fedayeen are killed and wounded in savage fighting that drives large numbers of Palestinians to seek refuge in Syria and Lebanon.

This slaughter of Arabs by Arabs is mourned by Palestinians as "Black September." A new terrorist group by that name is organized in Lebanon. Its sponsor is suspected to be Al Fatah, the largest Fedayeen group, led by Yasir Arafat. Black September's aims are to punish anti-Palestinian or pro-Israeli nations, to wage guerrilla warfare against Israel, and to win world headlines for Palestinian grievances by acts of terror.

In reprisal against Jordan, the Septembrists assassinate that country's prime minister, Wasfi Tal, when he visits Cairo in November 1971. Three months later they gun down five more Jordanian officials in West Germany. Letter bombs are mailed to Israeli diplomats all over the world, injuring postal workers as well as recipients. On May 8, 1972, the Septembrists skyjack a Belgian airliner in an attempt to force Israel to free Fedayeen prisoners in its jails.

The world is freshly shocked on May 30 when three young Japanese radicals, recruited by Black September, land at Israel's Lod Airport, whip out automatic rifles, and open fire on passengers. Twenty-four people are killed, eighty wounded. Most of the victims, ironically, are not Israelis but Puerto Ricans on a Christian pilgrimage to Jerusalem.

Black September's most sensational act of outlawry occurs on September 10 in Munich, where the Olympics are being held. Arab commandos break into the quarters of the Israeli Olympic team, assassinate two athletes and take nine others hostage. They demand that Palestinian prisoners in various countries be freed, and that a plane be provided to fly the terrorists to refuge in an Arab country of their own choice.

The West German government yields, but at the Munich airport police suddenly open fire on the kidnappers. The Arabs promptly blow up the nine hostages with hand grenades. Five Palestinians and one West German are also killed.

People everywhere are outraged and frightened. Where will Black September strike next? Who will be the next unsuspecting air passengers to be kidnapped in flight? How many people walking through air terminals will be suddenly and senselessly mowed down by Arab terrorists? How many secretaries opening mail will be blown to bits by letter bombs?

The Israelis are swift to retaliate. In September and November 1972 Israeli planes bomb Al Fatah camps in Jordan and Lebanon. Many Palestinian men, women and children are killed. In February 1973 Israeli fighter planes shoot down a Libyan civilian jetliner that strays over Israeli-occupied Egyptian territory in the Sinai Desert, killing one hundred eight passengers and crew.

On the same day Israeli marines and paratroopers attack two Palestinian refugee camps in Lebanon near Tripoli, killing thirty Arabs, including thirteen civilians. The Israelis accuse UNRWA, the UN Relief and Works Agency which administers the camps, of ''acting as host to a gang of terrorists.''

New acts of terrorism follow in bewildering confusion.

Black September pursues its goals by invading foreign embassies, holding some diplomats as hostages and killing others; by bombing Israeli ambassadors' homes; by skyjacking more airliners; by seizing foreign banks, taking hostages, and threatening to blow up the buildings; by hurling hand grenades into crowded airport transit lounges.

In reprisal for attacks on Israeli targets, the Israelis launch fierce raids on suspected Palestinian guerrilla bases in Arab countries, killing civilians along with commandos.

The Arab nations accuse Israel of standing in contempt of UN Security Council Resolution 242, passed after the Six-Day War, ordering Israel's armed forces to return behind its pre-1967 borders. Israel's refusal, Jordan charges, has "blocked all efforts towards a peaceful settlement in the Middle East, and forced the Arabs to resort to arms."

On October 6, 1973, as the Israelis celebrate their holy day of Yom Kippur, the armies of Egypt and Syria launch a surprise attack. Egyptian forces cross the Suez Canal and win back control of the east bank, while the Syrians capture considerable territory. The Israelis suffer heavy casualties, with large losses of planes, tanks, and equipment.

The jubilant Arabs do not really expect to crush the powerful Israeli army. They plan to fight only long enough to restore Arab pride, at low ebb since the defeat by Israel in the 1967 war, and to shock the great powers into compelling Israel to comply with UN Resolution 242.

After ten days of fighting the Israelis launch a powerful but costly counterattack. The Egyptians and Syrians are forced back until both their capitals are threatened with capture. Alarmed, five Arab oil-producing nations meet hastily in Kuwait on October 18 and reach decisions that frighten an oil-dependent world. An embargo is placed on oil deliveries to Israel's chief suppliers — the United States, Canada, and the Netherlands. Oil production will also be cut back five percent for every month Israel refuses to withdraw from occupied Arab territories and restore Palestinian rights.

The use of oil as a political weapon by Arab leaders compels the great powers to move swiftly to end the Yom Kippur War. The UN Security Council arranges a cease-fire, and negotiations begin for a peace settlement.

Pleased with their success in compelling the world to pay attention to Arab grievances, the Arab oil states remain united in a cartel — the Organization of Petroleum Exporting Countries (OPEC). To the consternation of the Western world, the cartel raises oil prices sharply. The era of cheap energy, OPEC tells the West, is over. Many nations heavily dependent upon oil fear bankruptcy. World inflation soars.

When peace talks are scheduled to take place in Geneva, the Palestinians are enraged at Israel's refusal to let them participate. Al Fatah guerrillas attack an Israeli apartment building in April 1974, killing eighteen people, mostly women and children. Another Fedayeen attack on an Israeli school in Maalot results in the deaths of twenty-one students. Israeli forces strike back with bombing raids on Lebanese refugee camps, killing fifty civilians, wounding two hundred, and wiping out one camp entirely.

Terrorism and counterterrorism escalate.

On October 14, 1974, the UN General Assembly votes to give Yasir Arafat and the PLO a voice in assembly deliberations, in effect recognizing the Palestinians as a legitimate government in exile. Two weeks later the heads of twenty Arab nations meet in Rabat, Morocco, issuing a call for the creation of an independent Palestinian state "on any Palestinian land that is liberated" from Israeli occupation. Arafat is recognized as the "sole legitimate representative of the Palestinian people."

This decision comes as a blow to King Hussein, who until

now has claimed the Palestinian West Bank occupied by Israel as part of his own kingdom. Despite the bitter war he had waged against the Palestinians four years earlier to compel them to recognize his authority, he now declares, "There is an Arab verse which says, in effect, where my tribe goes, I go."

Another deep-rooted Arab feud surfaces in April 1975 when a bus carrying Palestinian refugees winds through a Christian Arab section of Beirut, its passengers chanting PLO slogans. There is little love lost between the revolutionary Moslem PLO and the Christian, ultraconservative Phalangist party. Phalangist militia respond to the PLO taunts by opening fire on the bus, killing twenty-six Palestinians.

The incident sparks fierce religious warfare in Lebanon between Arab followers of the Cross and Arab believers in the Crescent. For over a year street fighting flares to the level of a brutal civil war that takes over five thousand lives.

The world is further appalled in April when the assassination of King Faisal of Saudi Arabia reveals another wide gulf between Arab and Western concepts of law and order. Saudi justice claims "a soul for a soul." Accordingly, the king's assassin, his young nephew, is publicly beheaded by an executioner's sword, with his head spiked and displayed to the crowd for fifteen gruesome minutes.

In July, Arafat vows to escalate the PLO's terrorist campaign in Israel, declaring, "We have our homes and our rights there, and we must recover them." Next day Palestinian commandos set off a bomb at busy Zion Square in Israeli-held Jerusalem, killing thirteen shoppers and wounding seventy-two. The blast, which hurls glass, debris, and bodies over a wide area, sets people's hair and clothing on fire, sending them screaming in pain through shocked crowds. As police round up Arab suspects, the maddened mob shrieks, "Kill them! Kill them!"

When United States Secretary of State Henry Kissinger negotiates a tentative peace treaty in September between Egypt and Israel, the PLO is outraged at Egyptian President Anwar Sadat for his "betrayal" of the Palestinian cause. In protest Fedayeen kidnap the Egyptian ambassador in Madrid, threatening to kill him if Sadat does not renounce the treaty. Sadat refuses, bitterly denouncing the terrorists, who do not carry out their threat.

The whirlwind of violence, counterviolence, and oil weaponry blowing out of the Middle East seems endless, upsetting a world longing for peace and security.

Most Westerners were bewildered by this sequence of events. It was difficult for them to distinguish between the various Palestinian movements, which ranged from educational to terrorist groups, and to know which were responsible for what.

"There is still too much fragmentation in our movement," acknowledged Mohammed Rashid, chief of foreign relations for Al Fatah, "and this has led to some tragic incidents that detract from the whole cause, things that a few individuals, acting independently, were responsible for."

At the same time he added, "We've taken up arms. Until we did that, we were ignored. Now the world is sitting up and paying a little more attention to what we seek."

In October 1972 Shafik Hout, head of the PLO office in Beirut, said, "We have to shock the West out of its guilty conscience about the Jews and into recognizing the plight of the Palestinian people." The attack on the Munich Olympics was a tactical success, he added, because it "showed we were prepared to die for our cause."

Arab spokesmen pointed out that world public opinion, outraged by Palestinian terrorism, had forgotten that before the

Zionists had been able to found the state of Israel, Jewish terrorist organizations like the Irgun and Stern gangs had committed similar acts of violence against Arabs and the British.

"We have reacted against the establishment of Israel on our land," said one Palestinian, "much as Americans might if the UN had turned Kansas and Oklahoma over to Vietnam refugees for a sovereign nation of their own, and the Vietnamese then had proceeded to drive out Americans and occupy their homes."

But Westerners were bewildered by the sudden intrusion of the distant Middle East crisis into their personal lives. Arab decisions became of crucial importance to shivering householders who faced cold furnaces in January and February of 1974, and to out-of-gas motorists searching for service stations that had not closed down as a result of the OPEC oil boycott. The Western world was further angered when huge price jumps for Arab oil touched off intolerable price increases for many other things needed in daily life.

These hardships intensified existing anti-Arab prejudice.

"Israel is seen as a 'Western' state populated by technologically minded, energetic, democratic, pioneering frontiersmen who are transforming a wilderness and providing a home for the persecuted,"observed Professor Malcolm H. Kerr, University of California political scientist. "The Arabs are seen as exasperatingly inscrutable, unreliable, inept, backward, authoritarian and emotional."

In some Western eyes the Arabs were also guilty of gross ingratitude. Where would they be if Western oil companies had not found and pumped their oil, applied modern technology to their backward economies, rescued them from sandy poverty by marketing their oil, and shared profits with their leaders? Was the price gouging of the OPEC cartel to be the West's reward for its help? This viewpoint ignored the role of Western oil companies as full partners in Arab oil, participating in the enormous profits extracted from Western consumers.

The Western image of Arabs was further confused by the Arab love of rhetoric, especially in zealous public avowals of dedication to sacred causes. Thus, before the 1967 Six-Day War, Egyptian President Gamal Abdul Nasser publicly vowed, in a moment of bluster and bravado, to drive the Israelis into the sea. His threat was taken literally in the West.

Arabologists considered Nasser's boast to be primarily political posturing to delight Egyptian nationalists, much as Premier Nikita Khrushchev played to a Russian gallery when he boasted in a word-joust with an American adversary, "We will bury you!" But Nasser's overblown rhetoric was as costly to the Arabs in terms of Western public opinion as Khrushchev's had been to the image of the Russians. Both leaders later claimed that their remarks had been misunderstood.

Israel was far more skillful in presenting its case to the West than the Arabs who, legally at least, had a more valid claim to world support. Palestinian despair had driven the Fedayeen to spotlight the Arab cause by headline-winning acts of terrorism, and those acts only provoked world revulsion.

Public opinion in the United States became so anti-Arab that when Kissinger angrily hinted in 1975 of the possibility of American military intervention in the Mideast to seize Arab oil fields, if OPEC did not lift its boycott and lower prices, many Americans were ready to support such an imperialist policy, despite the bitter experience in Vietnam.

Beset by vexing inflation, energy shortages, unemployment, and threats to world peace, most Americans and Europeans saw the Arabs only as callous terrorists or greedy oil barons.

The full truth about ninety-two million Arab people, of course, had little to do with such simplistic stereotypes.

# 2

# Through Arab Eyes

IT IS EASIER for an American to understand an Englishman, Frenchman, German or even a Russian than an Arab, because of our greater familiarity with European culture. The little we know of the Arabs and what they think is often inaccurate, moreover, because we tend to base our concepts on the words or deeds of a few Arab leaders or groups.

"Part of the Arab case against the West is that they cannot get through," observed the *New York Times Book Review* in 1968. "The communications are blocked or so it seems to them. They see themselves in the same situation as any other non-European people subjected to European colonization and the force of European arms, but their situation is not recognized. . . . Their Zionist opponents seem to control all the lines to liberal world opinion. . . . There will have to be some penetration of world opinion by the Arab . . . point of view."

In their often violent struggle to compel world attention to Palestinian grievances, the Arabs have been dismayed by Western denunciations of them as unfit members of the civilized world community. They resent being portrayed as a backward people unrealistically refusing to accept the permanence of an advanced Western nation that has thrived in their midst for better than a quarter of a century.

Arabs felt especially humiliated by the contemptuous jokes leveled at them in Western political cartoons and on TV, after their defeat in the 1967 Six-Day War, ridiculing them as an absurd people who "talked up a storm" but "couldn't fight their way out of a paper bag."

They have long been embittered by the scornful Western image of them as uncouth, ignorant Bedouin tribesmen who take savage joy in killing, of no world consequence except for the oil beneath their sands. In the Western media, the Israelis have generally been represented as the good cops of the Middle East, the Arabs as the robber bandits.

In their own view of Israel, the Arabs do not all agree on the future role they want for their Jewish neighbors. Radical Arab forces want Israel transformed into a Palestinian state under Arab control. Conservatives are willing to see Israel survive as a smaller nation, with land captured since 1967 given back to establish a Palestinian homeland.

Some Arabs oppose such a compromise settlement for fear that the Israelis, with their technological and economic superiority, would inevitably dominate the Arab nations on her borders. Others welcome it, seeking an economic union with Israel that would help develop the poorer Arab countries.

For centuries Arab self-respect has suffered because of powerlessness in the face of a superior weaponry that imposed alien rule on the Middle East. Frustration over such weakness helps explain the explosive nature of Arab protest. Most Arab adults grew up in a world they felt was beyond their control, forced to submit to foreign powers.

For these reasons, the Arabs are wary of any peace settlement in the Middle East imposed by the superpowers. They welcome big power interference only to the extent it is able to pressure Israel into yielding to Arab demands.

The average Arab is suspicious of *all* governments, including his own. "The camel has his concerns," says an old Arab proverb, "and the camel-driver his." Most Arabs tend to see government as a repressive force, and live their lives outside the government apparatus. Loyalties are given primarily to family, tribe, and the religious community of Islam.

This gulf between the leaders and the led exists even in revolutionary Arab states, where a left-wing military elite has seized power and sought to organize the masses around goals of rapid social change. The leaders can often whip up emotional street demonstrations, but find it more difficult to persuade their people to work hard toward distant national goals.

"Take care of today," the Arabs believe, "and let Allah take care of tomorrow." Nevertheless, some left-wing Arab regimes have been able to make social progress. In 1910, for example, Egypt had no public schools. Following the 1952 revolution, over five million students were enrolled in government educational institutions by 1970.

The concept of democracy is not a burning issue in the Middle East. Any Arab leadership is considered justified if it proves itself capable of governing well, and can manage to stay in power. "To him who has power over you," runs an old Arab maxim, "obedience is due."

Arabs are more concerned with democracy in personal rela-

tions. Although the Koran teaches acceptance of social differences ("We have created you in degrees, one above another"),
all Moslems must be visibly equal before Allah. They wear the
same clothes on pilgrimage, and are buried with equal simplicity. Those who lead the faithful in prayer are the most pious, not
the most important. Every Arab can approach Allah directly,
without the need of a priest intermediary. Theoretically he also
has the ear of his tribal or national leader, who must make time
to listen to his wishes or complaints.

Many Arabs believe that Western hostility toward them is in
large part animosity toward Islam as a rival of Christianity for
the allegiances of the world. They regard Christianity and
Judaism, despite the origin of both in the Middle East, as Western religions. Christian-Jewish differences are considered
merely a family quarrel, with both sects united when it comes to
dealing with the ninety-five percent Moslem Mideast.

Arabs regard Israel as a Judeo-Christian outpost implanted
by the West in the Middle East, both for imperialist purposes
and as a base for the conversion of Moslems. The West is uneasy, Arabs believe, because population changes have made
every fifth person in the world today a Moslem.

The Arab dream is that someday Moslem power can be unified and harnessed as a single great world force. Nasser once
wrote, "When I consider the 80 million Moslems in Indonesia,
and the 50 million in China, and the millions in Malaya, Siam
and Burma, and the nearly 100 million in Pakistan, and the more
than 100 million in the Middle East, and the 40 million in the
Soviet Union, together with the other millions in far-flung parts
of the world . . . I emerge with a sense of the tremendous pos-
sibilities which we might realize through the cooperation of all
these Moslems."

In the Arab view, Islam is the ultimate religion. Moslems believe that the word of God as reported by Moses was ultimately

corrupted, compelling God to send a new messenger, Jesus, to teach the Gospel. But when Christ's followers made the mistake of deifying the messenger, instead of worshiping God alone, God then chose Mohammed to correct this error. So Islam came into being, in the Arab view, as the final true religion of the one God the Arabs call Allah.

Followers of all other religions are considered infidels. Arabs find it disturbing that they, the true believers who once established a great empire noted for its cultural achievements, should be mired in the backwaters of the twentieth century, while the infidels of Western civilization dominate world science, art, learning, communications, and business.

Most Arabs resent the West politically, but envy its affluent way of life. Arab leaders seek to modernize their countries in the Western manner, although some impose restrictions to avoid what the French call "Coca-Cola-nization."

Central to the Arabs' painful feeling of rejection by the West is the Western support of Israel. The Arabs are convinced that Israel is an expansionist threat to them, planning to take more and more land to accommodate Jewish immigration from all over the world. Sadat called Israel "a dagger thrust into the back of Egypt and the Arab world."

Most Arabs support the decision of the 1967 Arab conference at Khartoum that there must be no recognition of Israel, no negotiations, and no peace, until the Palestinian refugees are restored to their homeland under their own government. Arabs also insist that Jerusalem, which contains the Dome of the Rock, the second most important Moslem shrine after Mecca, must be returned by Israel to Islamic control.

Arab leaders see the Israelis as modern Crusaders.

"Admittedly, I frequently called on Arabs to liquidate the State of Israel and to throw the Jews into the sea," acknowledged PLO spokesman Ahmed Shukairy. "I said this because I was—and still am—convinced that there is no solution other than the elimination of the State of Israel and the expulsion of all Palestine Jews from Palestine.''

On the other hand Arafat, as head of the PLO, declared, "When we achieve victory, we will never throw anybody into the sea! . . . We welcome with sincerity all the Jews who would like to live with us in sincerity in an Arab state as citizens having rights before the law and constitution.''

Almost all Arabs indignantly deny that they are anti-Semitic, insisting that their opposition to Israel is purely political, directed against the Zionists, not the Jewish people. "It is significant," acknowledged Professor Morroe Berger, director of Princeton's Near Eastern Studies Program, "that the wave of swastika-painting on synagogue walls in Europe and America in 1959-60 did not spread to the Arab world, except to Beirut, the Arab city with the highest proportion of Christians.''

When Hitler began persecuting the Jews of Europe, it was in the Arab world that most refugees sought sanctuary. Ironically, it was the establishment of the state of Israel by the Zionists that upset harmonious Jewish-Arab relations.

"It was not the Palestinian Arabs who ignited the ovens of Tierenstadt and Pilsen, of Dachau and Buchenwald," pointed out Professor Nabih A. Faris, American University of Beirut historian. "Why should the Arabs of Palestine pay for the crimes of Hitler? . . . Why dispossess the Palestinian Arabs in order to rehabilitate the victims of European fanaticism?''

Arnold Toynbee, noted historian of the Royal Institute of International Affairs in London, observed of the establishment of Israel, "In Arab eyes this looks like a conspiracy among the Western nations to salve the West's guilty conscience towards the Jews by compensating the Jews at the Arabs' expense. . . . What is to happen to the Jewish settlers on Arab land that has been seized forcibly, and without being paid for, since 1948?

'England and America created the problem; it is for them to solve it' is the Arabs' logical but unconstructive reply."

In the Arab view, if land had to be stripped away to make a refuge for homeless Jews, that land should have been taken from the guilty Germans, not from the Middle East.

"I will never accept that a person whose grandfather was converted to Judaism in Russia is automatically an Israeli simply by landing at Lydda Airport," said Professor Usama Khalidi, an Arab biochemist, "while I cannot go back to Jerusalem where I was born and raised until kicked out in 1948. How can Israeli intellectuals justify this injustice?"

"For twenty-two years the Palestinians have been uprooted and exiled in a new Diaspora [scattered colonies of a deported people] of their own," said Mohammed Rashid, chief of foreign relations for Al Fatah. "We're the new Jews, if you will. It's only normal that we should have become violent, if only mentally."

"By displacing the Palestinians," said Palestinian lawyer Henry Cattan, a former UN negotiator, "the Israelis put a time bomb in the foundations of their state. Either we defuse it together or one day it will explode."

Arabs reject the Zionist argument that the Jews had a right to return to their ancient homeland of Canaan, pointing out that ever since the dispersion of the Jews from Judea in A.D. 135, they had been only a small minority in Palestine thereafter. In Arab eyes the claim that the territory of Jerusalem rightfully belongs to the Israelis is as invalid as attempts would be to revive the Roman Empire, the Arab Empire, or the empire of Charlemagne. One Arab diplomat asked an American official at the UN, "If the United States believes in the rights of original settlers, when do you plan to give your country back to the Indians?"

Arab intellectuals are also bitter because the British permitted the Zionists to establish Israel in violation of a previous pledge to Arab leaders that Palestine would be given its independence as an Arab state. Only this pledge had won Arab consent for Jewish immigration to Palestine.

One Western argument that infuriates Arabs is the claim that Israel is more entitled to the disputed land because it is more progressive and "made the deserts bloom." According to that logic, Arabs point out, the technologically advanced United States should be entitled to take over Mexico and Latin America, while Canada should swallow Greenland, and South Africa should annex the undeveloped countries around it.

The Arabs also resent the readiness with which the Western press accepted the Israeli version of why Palestinians left their homes during the Middle East fighting. Zionists claim that the Palestinians were asked to stay by the Israelis but left, either voluntarily or because Arab leaders told them to. The Arabs insist that many were forced out by the Israelis, or fled in fear of Israeli acts of terrorism.

"Very seldom did I come across any reprimand of Israel or the Israelis [in the American press] without an accompanying justification," noted Dr. Michael W. Suleiman, Palestinian political scientist teaching at Kansas State University. "Only occasionally is the Arab point of view presented, and even then it sounds strange and unconvincing to a reader who has been saturated with the pro-Israeli stance."

Dr. Edward Said, an American humanist of Palestinian ancestry who teaches at Columbia University, pointed out biased terminology in news reports of Mideast affairs: "Although Israel illegally occupies a vast amount of territory, Arabs who resist the occupation are 'terrorists' rather than 'resistance fighters,' or even 'guerrillas.' "

Arab critics charge that when the 1967 war broke out, the American media confused the issue of who attacked whom. The press also defended Israel's occupation of Arab territory taken during the war on grounds that expanded frontiers were necessary for Israel's security. Jordan-born Kamel Abu-Jaber, an associate professor in government at Smith University, observed, "Israeli families are establishing settlements in the occupied territories — an action which the American news media regard as illustrative of the Israeli 'pioneering spirit.' "

Many Arabs resent the impression left by the American news media that all Mideast terrorism stems from the Arab camp. According to Dr. Israel Shahak, chairman of the Israeli League for Human and Civil Rights in Tel Aviv, since 1948 the Israelis have completely destroyed 385 Arab villages in fighting, forcibly removing men, women, and children from their homes. When an Arab village was attacked, Dr. Shahak reported, often every house, garden wall, and cemetery was demolished to prevent the return of fugitives.

Many displaced Palestinians are bitter because they have received no compensation for their lost property, and because friends or relatives are being held in Israeli jails on suspicion of belonging to Fedayeen groups.

Arab indignation over unjust treatment of the Palestinians is one side of the coin; resentment of Western disdain for Arabs is the other. Nasser once described his greatest problem as how "to restore dignity to Egypt." Arabs have never forgotten nor forgiven their humiliation by the Western powers during the nineteenth and twentieth centuries.

"I honestly don't believe the Americans make much effort to understand us, to make contact," Sheikh Abdulla Tariki, an American-trained geologist in Saudi Arabia, complained of ARAMCO oil officials. "They surround themselves with barbed wire to keep out the wild animals, including the human variety. And if they make use of the educated Saudi Arab they often put him somewhere where he can't make good. . . . To me it looks like a way of developing in the Arab a feeling of inferiority."

A strong desire to compel Western respect helped fuel the guerrilla warfare of the Palestinians, the Yom Kippur War begun in 1973 by Egypt and Syria, and the use of Arab oil to force the West to acknowledge Arab power.

Today's educated Arabs want the West to recognize that the "traditional" Arab — the uneducated, primitive Bedouin — is a vanishing breed. As a stereotype he is gradually becoming as obsolete as the image of Uncle Tom has become for American blacks.

Arab leaders today seek to borrow the trappings of modern Western life while retaining the best of their own traditions. Their goals include reducing poverty, illiteracy, and disease; building industries to provide jobs and a better standard of living; and establishing strong armies with modern weapons to participate in the international power struggle.

At the same time they are aware that changes wrought in Westernizing their world have already affected the Islamic culture, weakening parental authority, loosening family ties, increasing the movement from village to city, and reducing religious belief. Some Arabs refer to the problem as "Mecca versus mechanization." Religion is gradually being relegated to a corner of Arab life, rather than being at its core.

In discussing the Arabs as one people, it would be a mistake not to recognize that they are divided by sharp national, cultural, and religious differences. Egypt has often been at bitter odds with Saudi Arabia, Iraq, and Syria. Syria has frequently clashed with Iraq, Jordan, and Lebanon. Within each country Sunnis, Shias, Christians, and other sects clash. Assumptions of superiority by Egyptians and Syrians make them disliked and resented by the rest of the Arab world.

To add to these complexities in trying to understand the Arabs, the Arab nature tends to be ambivalent and volatile, with swift changes of mood. The inconsistent behavior of Palestinians on the occupied West Bank baffled British correspondent David Pryce-Jones until he understood it better.

"West Bank activists will begin by denouncing the Jews and all their works," he reported. "They will elaborate this into recriminations of the Arabs for being so abject, blaming themselves exaggeratedly for their own faults and showing up everybody's behavior in the worst light — after which you are a friend, you may drop in whenever you please and treat their house as yours. So it ceases to be a surprise that someone who is on public record as wanting the death of every Jew in fact spends weekends at a kibbutz; or that someone else who is proud of Fatah connections takes loans from the Israelis."

Perhaps the most profound split in the Arab world today is that between nations with a socialist or revolutionary outlook, like Syria, Iraq, the Democratic Republic of Yemen, Libya, and Egypt, and those with a traditional, conservative policy, like Lebanon, Jordan, Kuwait, and Saudi Arabia.

There are also revolutionary conflicts within some conservative Arab countries. In Oman, guerrillas of the People's Front for Liberation have been fighting its British-backed, oil-rich sultan since 1965. A twenty-nine-year-old, Sorbonne-educated Lebanese, Heiny Srour, trekked across two hundred fifty miles of desert and mountain to spend six months with the PFLO making a documentary film of their revolution.

"I made it for the Arab world," she explained, "because there is a total conspiracy of silence about this revolution. The opposing forces . . . control the mass media." Her film has been banned in most Arab countries as too radical.

Yasir Arafat felt that the support his own guerrilla movement received from the Arab world was too often limited to giving the Palestinians lip service unmatched by deeds.

"Our country has been occupied," he pointed out. "The

majority of our people have been kicked out by Zionism and imperialism from their homes. We waited and waited for the justice of the UN, for the justice of the world . . . while our people were suffering in tents and caves. . . . The only way to return to our homes and land is the armed struggle."

Two major developments are working for change in the Middle East—the use of oil to achieve world power and a better Arab standard of living, and the blend of seventh-century Islam with twentieth-century socialism. But beneath those modern forces ancient traditions still dominate Arab life. We need to appreciate those traditions if we are to understand Arab thought and behavior.

# 3

# These Are the Arabs

THE NAME Arab conjures up in Western minds such diverse images as the Sheikh of Araby, the savage infidel fought in the Crusades, the noble desert chieftain glamorized by Lawrence of Arabia, the thieving merchant of the bazaar, the Oriental sultan and his harem, the political terrorist, the oil tycoon.

For a more realistic view of today's Arabs, it is first necessary to ask, "Who is an Arab?" Originally, an Arab belonged to one of the nomadic tribes of the Arabian Peninsula. The ancient Jews knew them as Ishmaelites, descendants of Ishmael. The Bible refers to Ishmaelites as camel-breeding desert traders and warriors.

The rise of the Arab Empire after Mohammed, however, changed the concept of Arabism. New millions were added to the ranks of the original Arabs through conquest, Islamic conversion, intermarriage, and adoption of the Arabic language and customs. Today an Arab is considered to be anyone who lives in an Arab land, speaks the Arabic tongue, takes pride in Arab culture and traditions, and regards himself as an Arab.

This includes primarily Libyans, Egyptians, Sudanese, Jordanese, Palestinians, Syrians, Iraqis, Saudi Arabians, Yemenese, Kuwaitis, Bahrainese, and others who live in the tiny sheikhdoms of the Arab Peninsula. Moroccans, Algerians, and Tunisians are also considered Arabs, but more distant kin because of their remote position on the western fringe of the Middle East, and their strong ties to French culture.

The Arab countries form a loosely connected geographical unit, not unlike the nations of Europe. The Moslem religion is a strong bond that unites them, but it is not the determining factor of Arabism. There are Christian Arabs, and there are also hundreds of millions of Moslems who are not Arabs, like the Iranians, Turks, Indonesians, and Indians. Only one in six of the world's Moslems speaks Arabic.

For the eighty-five percent of Arabs who are Moslems, religion is part of daily life. Prayers are required five times a day — at dawn, midday, midafternoon, sunset, and nightfall. "Prayer is better than sleep!" the muezzin cries in the cold hours before dawn. As his call echoes from the minaret, the devout purify themselves by cleansing faces, hands, and feet with water or sand, then turn to face Mecca. Kneeling on a prayer rug, they touch forehead to ground and chant reverently, "There is no God but Allah, and Mohammed is his Messenger."

Moslem means, literally, one who submits or is resigned to the will of Allah, and Moslem rituals provide a feeling of personal security for Arabs, giving their lives a reassuring routine and regularity, and making them confident of a blissful afterlife. Fatalism is a recurring theme in the Islamic holy book, the Koran, which declares, "Nothing can befall us but what God hath destined. . . . No people can forestall or retard its destiny. . . . It is not for a believer, man or woman, to have any choice in their affairs, when God and His Apostle have decreed a matter."

Religious resignation has made reform and progress in the Arab world painfully slow. Of what use is it to struggle against misery or resist unjust rulers, if Allah in His divine wisdom has willed this state of affairs?

The Koran enumerates "five pillars" of Islam — the religious obligations of Moslems to (1) profess the faith; (2) pray; (3) give alms; (4) fast during the month of Ramadan; (5) make a pilgrimage to Mecca at least once, if possible.

The Koran also instructs Arabs in the conduct of their daily lives, prohibiting gambling, drinking, and eating pork. One of the more unusual taboos is the prohibition against making images of anything that has life, to prevent any possible lapse into idolatry. This taboo has compelled Arab artists to pour all their talents into creating beautiful arabesques — intricate, abstract patterns of color and shape which adorn Arab architecture. Despite the Koran, some modern Arab societies allow painting and sculpture, and teach conventional art in their schools. But Arab chessmen are abstract pieces, rather than the conventional figures of king, queen, knights and bishops. And in Riyadh, Saudi Arabian traffic signs indicate pedestrian crosswalks by human symbols minus heads.

There are three main classes of Arabs — the desert-dwelling Bedouin, the agricultural fellahin, and the city Arabs.

Bedouin are sometimes called "the Arabs of the Arabs" — the original Arabs of history, picturesque nomads who followed their animals around desert pasturage, raiding villages when the desert failed to provide their needs. They live harsh lives, enduring blazing heat, suffocating sandstorms, and raging desert winds to eke out a perilous, if wild and free, existence. The Bedouin are considered old at forty.

Their simple life has changed little in fifteen hundred years. The Bedouin male is clad in a knee-length shirt covered by an ankle-length robe, with a cord-tied head shawl wound around his neck and face to protect him against the fierce desert sun and keep sand out of his nose and mouth. His portable dwelling is a tent of camel- or goat-skin. Reserving water for his beasts, he lives on dates, flour, and camel or goat milk. For other food and essentials he barters surplus livestock.

The camel is the essential partner of the Bedouin, his "gift from Allah." It provides not only transport and milk, but also dung for cooking fuel. When this ship of the desert can no longer serve as a beast of burden, it becomes a Bedouin meal, and its skin serves to make a new tent or patch an old one. No other animal is so suited to the life of "the people of the camel," particularly since it can endure the heat without water for twenty-five days in winter, five days in summer. In a crisis a camel can also be made to spew up drinkable water for a parched Bedouin.

The Bedouin sees the desert as an inland sea, and moves across its vast wasteland with infinite patience, taking his flocks to feed wherever grass springs up in the changing seasons. Tenacity and endurance enable him to survive in a hostile wilderness where almost everything else perishes.

A rugged individualist, the Bedouin largely ignores governments, reserving his loyalty for his clan and tribe. The clan is the basis of Bedouin society. Every tent represents a clan. Related clans grouped together make a tribe. Water and pasturage belong to the tribe, but tents and household property are individually owned.

The tribes are governed by sheikhs who inherit their authority, subject to supervision by a council of elders. The sheikh is considered less a ruler than a respected arbitrator, and is addressed democratically by first name. Every tribal member has the right to approach him to offer or ask advice, or to seek redress of grievances.

Bedouin women are relegated to a subordinate role. They are expected to care for the animals and manage the household, family property, and children, while their husbands and fathers take coffee breaks that sometimes last all day. Sipping from cups in the shade of tents, the men offer hospitality to any who come by the encampment.

"Show kindness to your neighbor who is a stranger and your familiar companion and the traveler," orders the Koran. Westerner or Moslem on a pilgrimage, any traveler is welcome to stay up to three nights with a Bedouin family. No one knows better than the Bedouin the rigors of the desert.

Even more than most Arabs, the Bedouin live by an intensely emotional code of honor. "No Arab will ever forget a gesture of friendship; likewise he will always remember an act of hostility," observed Anthony Nutting, former British minister of state for foreign affairs. "No race on earth will more eagerly or cheerfully cut off its nose to spite its face. If their dignity is offended or their trust betrayed, the Arabs will react or retaliate without thought of the consequences."

The law of the desert, where there are no courts or jails, is "an eye for an eye, a tooth for a tooth." Blood feuds between clans may last for as long as forty years. An early Arabic poem expresses the fierce Bedouin spirit: "With the sword I will wash my shame away,/Let God's doom bring on me what it may!"

No Arabs are prouder of their heritage than the Bedouin, whose tribal history is carefully handed down in heroic verses recited from generation to generation. Although most Bedouin are illiterate, their command of spoken Arabic makes them eloquent. Their poetry is rich in imaginative beauty.

Bedouin verses stir listeners by evoking images of ancient

desert glory — great tribal victories in desert wars, valiant deeds of Bedouin heroes in billowing robes, dramatic struggles of Bedouin travelers against the terrors of the desert. The Bedouin take special pride in their centuries-old reputation for ferocity, which was well deserved.

One nineteenth-century explorer, Charles Doughty, observed, "Great is all townsmen's dread of the Bedouin, as if they were the demons of this wild waste earth."

But today's Bedouin are becoming an endangered species, rendered archaic by changing times. Some are turning into farmers and village-dwellers, lured from the desert by educational opportunities for their children or by part-time jobs. Only an estimated million or so Bedouin are left in all Arab lands, dwindling into legends like knights or cowboys.

Their last stronghold is Saudi Arabia, where the late King Faisal spent huge sums to provide water for Bedouin sheep, to tempt the tribes to settle down on five-acre farms. The plan failed because most Bedouin, too restless to remain in one place long, proved allergic to regular work.

"Trade the whole world for a garden? Never!" declared one Saudi sheikh. "And what would happen to our camels? They give us the milk of life and hair for our rugs. They carry us and our burdens without complaint. They are our freedom."

Many Bedouin, however, have become business partners of the farmers, who employ them to graze the farmers' livestock and transport their harvests on camelback.

The Bedouin are significant in today's Arab world primarily because of the spirit they represent — the desert traditions of independence, bravery, endurance, pride, vengeance, generosity, courtesy and hospitality.

The peasant, or fellahin, is the indispensable middleman of the Arab world, growing wheat to feed city Arabs and also the Bedouin in time of drought. The fellahin's roots go back much further than the Bedouin's, perhaps some ten thousand years to the first agricultural experiments in the Middle East. In today's Arab world, two out of three people are farmers. A typical Arab village consists of a group of windowless stone, adobe, mud, or thatch houses with a few shops, surrounded by farms. Nasser once described the village of Kafr el Baktikh as "the true Egypt." Its twenty thousand illiterate fellahin lived in brick houses and mud huts without electricity or piped water. In addition to a mosque, the village had one grocer, one doctor, one barber, and one primary school. The poorest fellahin families had the most children, averaging seven per family.

Most fellahin sleep on the floor, on reed mats, and often share their homes with cattle. Furnishings are sparse — a large box, a few old oil lamps, a small oil stove. Work begins at sunrise and ends at sunset, and wrests barely enough food from the soil for survival. Only a fraction of Arab land is arable, and water rights are often a matter of life and death. The fellahin dream not of ancient Arab glories or regaining Palestine, but of pumps and tractors.

The largest number of fellahin own their own small farms, but many are tenants, sharecroppers, and day laborers.

The Arab city dweller sometimes considers himself the most typical Moslem, because Islam began as a city culture. From seventeen to twenty-five percent of Arabs live in Middle East cities.

Most Arab cities are ancient, with modern new quarters built adjacent to and around them. The old section is the medina — a collection of neighborhoods built around specific trades, family groups, or religious factions. The medinas have degenerated into slums in whose narrow, serpentine alleys the city's historical treasures are to be found, along with the craft bazaars and dwellings of the poor.

The new section features broad avenues lined with fine shops, European-style buildings, luxurious tourist hotels, modern theaters, business and government offices. Built around the new city are some small factories, and the homes and shops of middle-class Arabs. In new suburbs further out one finds modern apartment buildings and villas for the upper middle class, the wealthy, and foreign residents.

Perhaps no Arab city blends past and present more strikingly than Cairo, Egypt. Its great hotels, apartment houses, and sky-scrapers intermingle with ancient mosques, museums, and universities in the shadow of the Pyramids. Cairo's broad avenues and winding side streets overflow with Arabs in sandals and long white *djellabas* who eat, trade, and even sleep in the streets.

Moslems are divided into no less than seventy-two sects, but the vast majority are orthodox Sunnis who stress their dedication to the path (*sunna*) of the Prophet. About twenty-eight percent are dissident Shias, who believe that the wrong caliph succeeded Mohammed. They are followers of the party (*shi'a*) of Ali, Mohammed's son-in-law, who they believe will return to earth and lead the faithful to new conquests and glory. The Shias represent the counterculture of the Moslem world, and are often identified with non-Arab Moslems. Christian Arabs, a very small minority, are found chiefly in Lebanon.

All Moslem Arabs recognize an obligation to respond to the call for a *jihad,* or holy war on infidels, when it is made by recognized religious authorities. Yet in practice Islam has been far more tolerant of other religions and nationalities than Christianity. For centuries after the establishment of the Islamic Empire, conquered peoples were permitted to retain their own schools, languages, and religious practices.

If Islam unites the Arab nations, their political differences divide them. Arab governments range from feudal monarchies

like Saudi Arabia to democracies like Lebanon, socialist republics like Egypt, and left-wing dictatorships like Syria. The
struggle among them for power is fierce and uncompromising.

Arab leaders have gone to great lengths to plot each other's
assassinations. "King Saud of Saudi Arabia was accused of
spending several million dollars," noted the United States National Commission on the Causes and Prevention of Violence,
"in an abortive attempt to kill Nasser." The present kings of
Saudi Arabia and Jordan occupy their thrones because their
fathers were assassinated. Egypt's intelligence officials charge
Libya's Muammar Qaddafi with plotting to murder Sadat.

Despite frequent lip service given to the goal of pan-Arab
unification, each Arab leader has a vested interest in separatism.
He is wary of yielding any of his own power to the Arab
League; he distrusts ambitious rivals he suspects of either seek-
ing to become sultan of a new Arab Empire, or selling out the
Arab cause to the West for national advantage.

The people of each Arab country have their own distinct national characteristics. Saudi Arabians, cut off from other Arabs
outside the harsh, forbidding Arabian Peninsula, tend to be the
most insular, traditional, and devout. It is their desert country
that contains the holy shrines of Mecca and Medina to which
over a million Moslems flock from all over the world in an annual pilgrimage.

Mostly nomadic Bedouin herdsmen, these largely illiterate,
racially unmixed Sunni Moslems are loyal to a paternalistic
monarchy that allows no political parties, no elections, no legis-
lative bodies, and no radical movements.

The smaller states of the Arabian Peninsula — Kuwait,
Bahrain, Qatar, the United Arab Emirates, Oman, and the two
Yemens — are strung around Saudi Arabia like a necklace.
Most differ from the other Arab states in that their people —

fishermen, pearl divers, boat builders — have traditionally looked out to the sea, rather than inward to the desert for their livelihood. But the discovery of oil has made a vast difference for many of them.

Kuwaitis are among the most envied of Arabs because Emir (Prince) Sabah Al-Salim, made fabulously wealthy by oil revenues, has given his people a welfare state that provides them with free medical care, education, social security, and other government benefits. Perhaps because of their good fortune, Kuwaitis are reluctant to take jobs they consider demeaning — not only janitorial work and housework, but also nursing and carpentry.

Egyptians, who outnumber all other nationalities in the Middle East, are usually recognized as the most important bellwethers of the Arab world. "When a storm brews in Cairo," observed one Arab, "every Arab feels the breeze."

The principal concern of overcrowded Egypt is getting enough food to avoid famine. With over ninety-five percent of its land desert, most of its thirty-seven million people are jammed into a narrow farming zone on either side of the Nile. Annual income averages only a hundred dollars a year. The average fellah exists on only two thousand calories a day, far below the minimum needed for decent health. With disease rampant, life expectancy is only forty years.

Despite overwhelming problems, Egyptians maintain a wry sense of humor. When Sadat demanded that Israel return the captured east bank of the Suez Canal, one Egyptian wit suggested, "We'll get all thirty-seven million Egyptians together and march them to the canal. On a given signal, face to face with the enemy, all thirty-seven million of us will smile. Can you imagine how disarming it would be to look on thirty-seven million smiling Egyptians?"

Syrians are the most vocally militant of all Arabs, and their militancy is also directed against each other. The curse of Syria is sectarianism. Constant quarreling among over twenty different religious sects makes the country politically unstable. There have been incessant bloodless coups as one faction has ousted another from power.

Although ninety percent of Syrians are Moslems, they are divided into Sunni and Shia camps, with no less than ten different Christian sects among other minorities. Syria is divided further into regions with separate customs, folklore, manners, dress, and Arabic pronunciation.

The dominant Syrian party is the Baath (Arab Socialist Renaissance), which is dedicated to resurrecting the glories of the Arab Empire and restoring Arab racial purity. Despite several attempts, Syrians have found it impossible to get along with the Egyptians in a combined republic.

The Israelis have no more bitter enemy. Sheltering over 140,000 Palestinian refugees, the Syrians ardently support all PLO Fedayeen attacks against Israel. Antagonistic to the West, the Syrians look to the Soviet Union for military aid.

Like the Syrians, Iraqis have sharp differences among themselves. Some ninety-five percent are Moslems, over half of them Shias. Minorities include Christians, Kurds, Yezidis, Assyrians, Jews, sun-worshipers, and devil-worshipers. The Kurds are Sunnis who seek independence. "The regime decided that the best way to deal with us," said Kurd guerrilla warrior Mulla Mustafa Barzani, "was to wipe us off the map."

Unlike Syrian coups, changes of regime in Iraq are usually bloody. The Baath party presently in power seeks to modernize the country through Soviet aid. "This does not mean that we are a satellite of any other socialist country," insisted Mohammed Jamil Shalesh, Iraqi information minister. "In some ways we may be more socialistic than Russia. But ours is an Arab socialism; atheist politics we could never abide."

Most Jordanians are Sunni Moslems, divided into urban dwellers, farmers, and Bedouin herdsmen. They have diverse backgrounds since the area they occupy was once part of Syria, then Turkey, and is now crowded with Palestinian refugees. Jordan was a geographical creation of Britain after World War II. Ever since, it has been dependent on Western loans, making King Hussein suspect in many other Arab leaders' eyes.

The Lebanese are the best educated, most politically sophisticated and Westernized of the Arabs, world-famous as shrewd traders. The story goes that if a Lebanese boy is asked how much are two and two, he asks, "Are you buying or selling?"

Like the business-minded Swiss, the Lebanese prefer the commercial advantages of neutrality in the world's quarrels. Their prosperous ivory tower was badly battered in 1975 when civil war broke out between Christians and Moslems, upsetting the delicate balance of power between them.

Until savage fighting crippled Beirut as a banking and commercial center, the Western influence in Lebanon was pronounced. Coca-Cola signs and mosques were side by side. Gas stations were identified as Shell. Veiled women rode in Chevrolets and Citroens. Mini-skirted girls went to American films and bought books imported from New York, London, and Paris.

Significantly, of over a million Arab-speaking immigrants and their descendants who now live in the United States, about ninety percent are Christians from Lebanon. Some seventy thousand live within the Detroit area, working for the auto companies.

In Lebanon both Moslems and Christians carry *misbaha* beads, known as "worry beads," intended to help count the number of times a prayer has been recited. Shrewd Lebanese study the way in which an Arab fiddles with his *misbaha* for a clue to his mood, the tempo of clicks suggesting whether he is bored, nervous, impatient, or angry.

The Palestinians number some 2,775,000, only 350,000 of whom still remain in Israel proper. The rest are scattered as refugees throughout the Arab world. The greatest number, 700,000, are in Jordan, with an almost equal number in the Israeli-occupied West Bank of Jordan. The Israeli-occupied Gaza Strip next to Egypt has 375,000, with 275,000 in Lebanon, 175,000 in Syria, 170,000 in Persian Gulf states, 25,000 in Egypt, and only 10,000 in Iraq. Many of the families are broken up; some relatives have not seen each other in over twenty years.

About a million and a half Palestinians are in squalid refugee camps supervised by UNRWA (UN Relief and Works Agency), living on handouts which demoralize their self-respect. They are understandably bitter, not only toward the West for having permitted Israel to occupy their homeland, but also toward Arab nations, which regard them as an irksome problem and would like to be rid of them.

"We Palestinians are buffeted by every wind that blows across the Arab world," complained an oil consultant in Beirut. "If Saudi Arabia and Egypt fall out, we pay the price. If Iraq and Syria are at odds, we are caught in the middle. If Moslem fights Christian in Lebanon, we suffer."

Most Palestinians support Fedayeen raids and guerrilla warfare, both in hopes of regaining their homeland and because striking such blows makes them feel less helpless.

The West tends to think of all Palestinians as either miserable illiterates in the UNRWA camps, or brutal terrorists armed with explosives, grenades, and rifles. Actually, hundreds of thousands are successful teachers, doctors, businessmen, civil servants, and technicians in many of the Arab countries where they now live. Some have even become millionaires.

Although Tunisians are mostly Moslems, divided between Arabs and Berbers, their leader, Habib Bourguiba, is a peace-minded reformer who once quit the Arab League in protest against its policies. He de-emphasizes Islam and Pan-Arabism, stressing Tunisian nationalism. "We are all Tunisians now," he told his people, "whether we are French or Arab, Christian or Moslem or Jew. We are all children of one country, and all of us must work together for the good of all."

Like Tunisia, Morocco operates largely outside the pale of the Arab world. Only a third of Moroccans are Arabs, with another third Berbers and the rest of various backgrounds. Most are Moslems, and speak and dress Arabic style. But a strong French influence keeps Morocco in a middle-of-the-road position between the Middle East and the West. To a large extent this is also true of Algeria, although both Algeria and Morocco are both members of the Arab League.

There are still further divisions within the Arab world, perhaps none greater than the barriers that separate Arab men from Arab women.

# 4

# Inside the Arab Family

MOST ARABS think of their homes as divided into public spaces for the use of the men and guests, and private or family spaces for the use of the women. Public rooms often have two entrances, so that if a male guest arrives unexpectedly the women of the family can slip out the other exit. The Islamic code requires as much isolation of women from males outside the family as possible.

"Stay in your houses!" the Koran instructs women. "Do not exhibit yourselves as women did in the early days of ignorance. . . . Let them show their charms only to their husbands or fathers." Most Arab women are veiled in public, but originally the veil was used as a mark of status; it was never worn by women of the Egyptian peasantry or the North African Bedouin.

Arabs who can afford it like as much open space in their

homes as possible, with high ceilings, an unobstructed view, and preferably an indoor skylit garden "for the soul." Dogs and cats as pets are considered dirty by Moslems, but tropical fish and birds are popular middle-class household companions.

In rural villages of the Middle East, Arabs generally live as self-sufficient family units. Households consist of a farmer, his wife or wives, their unmarried children, and their married children with partners and offspring.

Children are raised in exactly the same way their parents were brought up, although educated urban Arabs are substituting modern child-rearing methods for traditional patterns. Arabs take great pride in their children, and often live vicariously through them. There is little interest in limiting family size, despite great poverty. "Do not kill your children for fear of poverty," Mohammed quoted Allah. "We will feed them and you."

Islam makes it clear that a daughter is far less desirable than a son. "When the birth of a daughter is announced to a man," the Koran declares, "his face darkens. Choking, he turns away from his family in shame at what has been announced to him, wondering whether he will keep the child for his dishonor, or whether he will bury it in the dust." A girl is tolerated if she is firstborn, but each successive daughter born before the appearance of a son is considered a calamity.

"The women, no less than the men, consider a girl of little worth," observed sociologist Jean Duvignaud of the University of Tunis. "The midwife hardly dares tell a man that he is the father of a girl, whereas she runs joyfully to announce the birth of a boy. It is strange indeed, however, that the women should speak belittlingly of their own sex."

A girl is considered an inferior minor under her father's rule until he transfers his guardianship to her bridegroom. A wife is allowed only one husband, but her husband is allowed four wives and an unlimited number of concubines. This law, however, is at odds with general practice today. Few Arabs except the wealthy can afford more than one wife, and the practice is dying out among Westernized Arabs.

"Polygamy is now rare among the educated classes," noted Saudi Arabian official Hassan Yassin. "The Koran allows four wives — but all must be treated equally. Many of us believe it would be hard to do justice to more than one wife."

A woman's legal status in the Arab world is lower than a man's. She can inherit only half as much of her parents' estate as her brother. Her testimony in court is given only half the value of a man's. An interesting exception is found among the Bedouin, who accept a woman's unsupported word in charges of assault. The reason: Bedouin men want women free to move safely about the desert while tending flocks and drawing water.

Arab women are considered basically impure. According to Islam, a man becomes impure when he touches a woman or a dog. He must then purify himself by prolonged washing.

Men and women do not speak freely with one another except on university campuses, in modern business offices or other places where tradition is changing, and in those educated families that have adopted a Western social code.

In some Arab lands the man a girl marries is called her "fate." Girls are taught to regard the husbands selected for them by their fathers as a matter of destiny. Romantic love is not the basis of Middle East marriages, except among Bedouin women, who may select their own husbands if they wish. Often betrothals are made between cousins. In Iraq and Syria a girl can marry a "stranger," as a rule, only if no uncle has reserved her as a wife for his son.

Usually newlyweds live with the bridegroom's family, the bride falling under the total jurisdiction of her mother-in-law. Once she produces her first child, however, her status improves, particularly if she has a son, and she is gradually given more responsibility in the household.

In the villages husbands seldom bother to speak to their wives, placing little importance on what they think. What a husband wants principally from his wife are his meals prepared, his household managed, his sons created, and his honor unsullied. "Theirs are two separate worlds, which pass without touching," observed Duvignaud.

Women are expected to be docile marriage partners, submissive to their husbands. According to Mohammed, a home is accursed if a woman's voice can be heard outside its walls.

Until recently divorce in most Arab countries was a male privilege. A husband needed only say to his wife three times, in the presence of two witnesses, "I divorce you," and return her and any children under seven to her family. In many Arab countries today, however, divorce laws have been tightened.

The Arab woman of the village, desert tribe, or medina is secluded and guarded in the belief that she has strong sensual desires that can otherwise betray her. She is forbidden to discuss sex with a man, even her husband. Loss of chastity or infidelity are regarded as a severe disgrace meriting banishment or even death at the hands of a male family member.

In Cairo a nineteen-year-old man stabbed his sixteen-year-old sister to death after overhearing her whisper to her mother that she had been seduced. In Jidda, Saudi Arabia, a young couple found to be having an affair were buried to the waist in a public square and stoned to death. In upper Egypt, despite a minimum four-year prison penalty for such killings, if an unwed mother's male relatives do not slay her, a neighbor will sometimes volunteer to do it "for the honor of the village."

Sometimes a girl may pay with her life simply for violating the rules of social conduct. In Cairo a man turned himself in to a police station with a bloody knife in his hands, proudly announcing — to the cheers of a crowd following him — that he had caught his sixteen-year-old niece meeting secretly with a young man in the street, and had "washed away the dishonor" by slaying her with his own hands.

Frank Holmes, a New Zealand oilman, once said, "If I am ever reincarnated and sent back to Arabia, there are two things I would never want to be. A donkey — or a woman."

The women's liberation movement, nevertheless, has penetrated even the male chauvinism of the Islamic world. Progress is slow, but changes are taking place as more and more Arab women are emancipated by education and greater freedom to move outside the home. Many are now working in factories and shops alongside men, an innovation that only a few years ago would have been highly shocking to most Arab communities.

Public education for girls has become much more common in both cities and villages. Many girls and women are discarding the veil and traditional *djellaba,* or full-length Arab robe, for Western dress. The harem as an Arab institution has become increasingly rare.

Egypt is the principal Arab country seeking to bring about sexual equality. Egyptian women can now work as social workers, teachers, lawyers, surgeons, engineers, accountants, and research scientists. One in four members of the Journalists Union is a woman, and some of them are foreign correspondents.

In newly created Egyptian farm villages made possible by the irrigation of the Aswan Dam, some women are enjoying better lives than they have known in the past. There are schools for illiterate adults, day-care centers, cooperative stores, indoor toilets, running water, village TV, recreation centers, and birth control clinics.

In Kuwait upper-class Arab women may attend a dinner or social evening with European men, although they arrive at a host's house fully veiled. When the door closes behind them, they can then discard veil and cloak, and proceed in to dinner attired in the latest style of Western evening gown.

Perhaps the slowest Arab nation to change with regard to the position of women is Saudi Arabia, where women are forbidden to drive cars or work in the same offices as men. Syria acknowledges the right of women to enter the male working world, but by 1970 less than one percent of Syrian girls were receiving technical education, compared to ten percent in Egypt. The proportion of girls in Syrian universities is high for an Arab country — one in five students — but it has not changed in the last twenty years. "Most of the women in the Arab countries are oppressed, and I'm part of them," declared twenty-nine-year-old Heiny Srour, the Sorbonne-educated Lebanese film maker.

In the fall of 1974 Cairo held a conference on the role of the Arab woman in national development, attended by delegates from fifteen Arab countries. The delegate from Kuwait, Najat al-Sultan, declared that if the Arab world gets around to accepting the conference resolutions, "the wheel of change will be set forward. A new kind of woman would emerge, and then you would have a new kind of man, too."

Increasing contacts between the cultures of the West and Middle East have brought unsettling changes to the Arab world at an ever-swifter pace. Westernization has not only changed the face and traffic patterns of Arab cities, but has also affected family life, weakening parental authority and sparking a movement from village to city. Young Arabs educated in the West have returned home with needed technical skills which their countries welcome, but also with a reduced Islamic zeal, which disturbs Arab religious authorities.

Westernization has also brought significant change to the Bedouin. The governments whose lands they once roamed freely are now bringing them under increasing control. Swifter government mobility through cars, trucks, buses, and airplanes has also largely replaced the Bedouin's former policing function in the desert, and damaged the camel market.

Dwindling in numbers and importance, the Bedouin recognize unhappily that their time is passing, just as the Western pioneers who once were so vital a force in the American scene gradually vanished and became legends.

Many Arabs today welcome change but disagree on what kind, the extent, and how it is to be brought about, and who should direct it. Often their expectations are unrealistic.

Young Moroccan writer Driss Ben Hamed Charhadi recalled the euphoria in his country when the French were preparing to leave: "Everybody in the city was happy, everywhere in the streets. They were going to get their freedom. One man was saying: The Christians are leaving! I'm going to have a big house on the Boulevard, and it will be all mine. Mine! Another was saying: I'm going to be a commissaire! And they were all telling each other they were going to be rich, and no one would ever have to ask for alms in the street again. . . . But not one of them knew how to read or write."

Jamil Saliba, of the Institute of Higher Arab Studies in Cairo, observed that the Syrian and Lebanese farmer "often imagines things and believes that they really exist because they fit his feelings and dreams. . . . They ask the government to plant their deserts with figs and olives, to make their wells gush forth, to revive the land for them, and to guarantee their livelihood. But whenever they are called upon to work in cooperation, they object and each one prefers to do the work individually."

Despite a reluctance to cooperate, Arabs like to feel that they are part of one great Arab nation that supersedes national boundaries. This pride is fed to a large extent by the Arab League, a loose confederation of Middle East states formed by a common language and culture. These bonds do not prevent frequent quarrels, but the nations' common enmity with Israel holds the Arab League together. "He who is the enemy of my enemy," the Bedouin proverb goes, "is my friend." Whenever members of the League attempt to draw closer politically or geographically, however, the effort fails.

The inability to absorb many secondary school and university graduates into jobs they have been trained for is a serious problem for most Arab countries. Qualified young Egyptian engineers consider themselves lucky to get jobs like checking on street manhole covers to see that they are in place.

Expectations aroused but unfulfilled have created widespread dissatisfaction among millions of Arab youth, especially those educated abroad. They feel frustrated by the contrast between the Western world they have been living in, and the limited opportunities at home. Significantly, the victorious coups in Egypt, Syria, and Iraq were all led by young men — as much a clash of generations as of economic classes.

Another serious problem is the Arab glorification of fathering sons, which has led to serious overpopulation on poor land that cannot sustain such huge numbers. The standard of living for the masses remains distressingly low, with disease compounding the misery of poverty.

Despite the temptations of poverty, crime is not the serious problem for the Arab world that it is for us. Perhaps the reason is fear of the harsh punishment Islamic law prescribes for offenders. "If a man or woman steal," says the Koran, "cut off their hands in retribution of that they have committed." In cases of repeated theft, the foot is also to be amputated. If a man is convicted of either treason or murder, he may be decapitated.

"I've seen a dozen Arabs lose their hands for theft," declared an American ARAMCO technician in Saudi Arabia, "and I've seen men strung up bleeding in the street, and I've seen two decapitated." He found such severe punishment paradoxical among a people so pious they prayed five times a day. But from the Arab point of view, Western societies that treat convicted prisoners humanely encourage a high crime rate.

An important key to understanding the Arabs is their strong streak of emotionalism, which can be quickly aroused by the vivid imagery and persuasive force of the Arabic language. A people with a tradition of great lyric poets and eloquent talkers, Arabs accept exaggeration as a form of poetic license. A flight of brilliant or impassioned oratory may also overpower the more credulous into accepting rumor as fact, or word for deed.

Like many Western governments, including our own, Arab governments are not above lying to their people, when in the view of their rulers a distortion of the facts is necessary to win popular support. Embellishment of the truth is not considered a great sin in the Middle East. The Prophet himself approved of falsehood if it served any of three purposes — reconciling feuding persons, pleasing one's wife, or obtaining an advantage in a conflict with infidels.

"No people in the world have such enthusiastic admiration for literary expression and are so moved by the word, spoken or written, as the Arabs," noted Philip K. Hitti, professor emeritus of Semitic literature at Princeton. "Hardly any language seems capable of exercising over the minds of its users such irresistible influence as Arabic. Modern audiences in Baghdad, Damascus and Cairo can be stirred to the highest degree by the recital of poems only vaguely comprehended. . . . The rhythm, the rhyme, the music, produce on them the effect of what they call 'lawful magic.' "

Wherever the ancient Arabs went, they carried with them a passionate attachment to their language, intoxicating others by its beauty into adopting it. "The religion preserved the language," observed Rashid Rida, a modern Syrian writer, "and the language preserved the religion."

Modern European tongues — English, Spanish, Portuguese, French, and Italian — owe a debt to Arabic, borrowing many words from the language. In English the list is endless: algebra *(al-Jabr);* alcohol *(al-kuhl);* admiral *(amir al);* barrack *(barqa);* coffee *(gahwah);* genius *(genii);* ghoul *(ghul);* giraffe *(zirafah);* guitar *(qitar);* lute *(alud);* mare *(mahr);* mufti *(mufti);* orange *(naranj);* safari *(safara);* sandal *(sandal);* sugar *(sukkar);* tariff *(tarif);* and many others.

In today's Arab coffeehouses, village squares, and city marketplaces, *rawis,* or storytellers, follow an ancient tradition, mesmerizing audiences with tales of the bravery, strength, romances, shrewdness, and treachery of ancient Arab nobles. They are skilled performers who know how to keep their listeners in breathless suspense, drawing out gasps, laughter, and cries of admiration for the centuries-old heroes of their lyricism.

Although all Moslems glorify the past greatness of the Islam Empire, Arab nostalgia for bygone splendor is the most intense because that ancient glory was primarily Arabic.

"One cannot begin to understand the modern Arab," observed Professor Wilfred Cantwell Smith, director of McGill University's Institute of Islamic Studies, "if one lacks a perceptive feeling for this."

In the following pages we will see why the history Arab children are taught leads them to grow up yearning for a renaissance of the great days when the Arabs were indisputably the leading civilization on earth.

# 5

# The Days of Glory

THE ORIGINAL Arabs are considered descendants of an Arabian Peninsula tribe, the Sem, who settled in Yemen under the kingdom of Yarab in pre-Biblical times. (Sem gave us "Semite"; Yarab, "Arab," or desert-dweller.) About 3500 B.C. Semites migrated to Egypt, intermarrying with the Hamites to produce the Egyptian race. Another migration to the Tigris-Euphrates valley led to intermarriage with the Sumerians, producing the Babylonians. Subsequent migrations to Syria and Palestine produced the Amorites and Phoenicians.

The Jews were next-door neighbors of the Arabs, and racially kin. Moses married an Arab woman, daughter of a Midianite priest, who instructed him in their cult of Yahu (Yahweh, later Jehovah). Job, that model of Old Testament resignation to the will of God, was not Jewish but Arabic, according to Arab-ologist Philip K. Hitti in his book *The Arabs.*

The continual crossing of early Mideast cultures accounts for the similarity found in the languages of the ancient Arabs, Babylonians, Assyrians, Arameans, Chaldeans, Phoenicians, Amorites, Hebrews, and Abyssinians.

The first known record of the Arabian Peninsula and the Arabs is found in Genesis, where Arab people and districts are mentioned by name. The earliest identification we have of an Arab as such is an inscription by an Assyrian king, Shalmaneser III, who in 853 B.C. recorded a victory over the king of Damascus, noting the destruction of a thousand camels belonging to an enemy sheikh, "Gindibu the Arab."

The most important pre-Islamic kingdom in northern Arabia was Kinda, which prospered in the late fifth and early sixth centuries. Kinda united many Bedouin tribes of the peninsula, and developed a common language and poetic literature that were handed down orally through the generations. The three most esteemed talents were eloquence, archery, and horsemanship.

In the sixth century before Mohammed was born, Europe was steeped in the Dark Ages. The Roman Empire was overrun by barbarians. In the east the Byzantine Empire had been almost extinguished by long wars with the Persians. Arabia itself, despite the cultural advances of Kinda, was a primitive tribal society that worshiped idols and jinns, or demons.

The religion of the Bedouin nomads derived from the paganism of the ancient Semites — worship of a moon god and other gods living in trees, fountains, and sacred stones. Failure to worship the tribal god, a stone effigy carried around in a red tent guarded by the sheikh, was considered treason.

Monotheism existed in southern Arabia among some Christian and Jewish communities, but it held little interest for superstitious Arabs during what Moslems call the Jahiliyah period — the time of ignorance and barbarism.

Mecca, chief city of Hejaz in western Arabia, was little more than a large desert oasis. From A.D. 440 it was ruled by a merchant oligarchy, the tribe of Koraysh, descendants of Abraham and Ishmael. Mecca had grown rich as a key caravan station on land routes over which camels took the spices of Yemen north to Syria, and Persian silks west to the Nile.

Mecca also prospered as a pilgrimage center of idol-worshipers. The Koraysh were custodians of a shrine called Kaaba, purported to be the holy abode of three hundred sixty stone effigies of pagan gods and jinns.

Mohammed was born to a poor branch of the Koraysh tribe in Mecca around A.D. 570. His father died before his birth, and his mother when he was six. He was brought up by his uncle, the merchant Abu Taleb, who took him along on frequent caravan trips to Syria. At a Syrian monastery he was influenced away from idolatry by a Christian monk named Bahira.

At twenty-five Mohammed married a rich widow fifteen years his senior, Khadija, and used her money to enter the caravan trade. Just before his fortieth birthday, while meditating in the cool of a hill cave, he had a vision in which the angel Gabriel told him he had been chosen "the Prophet of Allah" (*al-ilah,* the one God). He felt himself instructed to transmit divine messages to the Arab people, just as Moses had to the Jews and Jesus to the Christians. For the next twenty years Mohammed continued to experience revelations which were later recounted as holy writ in the Koran, or Recitation.

Mohammed prophesied that on Judgment Day rich rewards in Paradise awaited those who submitted to Allah's will, while idol-worshipers who refused would suffer dreadful punishments in hell. It was the same message, basically, as that preached by the Judeo-Christian faith.

Mohammed's first converts were family members, then close friends. Meetings of the early Moslems were held in secret at first, out of fear of the Korayshites. The ruling merchants took alarm when the Islamic sect grew large, threatening to dismantle their profitable pilgrimage business built around the Kaaba. Branding Mohammed a troublemaker, they unleashed the Meccan army against the Moslems.

The Prophet was beaten and stoned, his disciples tortured. Forced to take his followers into exile, Mohammed brought them two hundred twenty miles north to Medina in what became known as the Hegira, the Year of the Flight (622). In this agricultural community of Arab and Jewish tribes, he sought to convert his fellow monotheists, the Jews, to Islam by adopting Jewish rituals like the fast of Yom Kippur, and the recitation of prayers facing Jerusalem, holy city of the Jews and Christians.

When the Jews rejected his claim to be God's prophet, Mohammed angrily dropped all Jewish practices, substituting Mecca, the site of his visions, as the direction of prayer.

After his wife Kadija died he took six more wives, each one binding him politically by marriage to an important tribe of Arabia. His favorite daughter, Fatima, married Mohammed's cousin Ali, an alliance that was subsequently to split the Moslem world into the Sunni and Shia sects.

Mohammed claimed a revelation that bade him "fight in the cause of Allah against those who fight against Him." This was his first call to *jihad* — holy war. Urging his followers to pick up their swords against the pagan Koraysh, he assured them that death would come only when Allah willed, so that they might as well fight unbelievers and assure themselves of a welcome in Paradise if they fell in battle.

When his forces defeated the ruling Omayyad tribe of Mecca in 630, Mohammed, wearing the pilgrim's white robe, led his followers to the Kaaba, where every one of the three hundred sixty stone idols was smashed. "Truth hath come," he cried, "and falsehood hath vanished!" From then on he forbade as idolatrous any pictures or statues reproducing the human form.

He began to unify the Arabian Peninsula under the banner of Islam. Some tribes were defeated and annexed, while others joined Mohammed voluntarily by paying *jizyah*, a poll tax.

In the tenth year of Hegira, forty thousand believers followed the Prophet to Mount Arafat on his final pilgrimage. Leading them in prayer as dawn broke over the mountain, he declared, "Oh, Lord, I have delivered thy message and accomplished my work." Returning from Mecca to Medina, he fell sick and, on June 8, 632, died in the arms of his favorite wife, Ayesha.

The cry with which Mohammed was buried—*La ilaha il-la' llah: Muhammadun rasulu-' llah!* (There is no god but Allah: Mohammed is the messenger of Allah!)—had largely unified the people of the Arabian desert. It was soon to send them riding from land to land, swords upraised, to collect hundreds of new souls for Islam. The chant became the first and last words a Moslem heard in life, and the refrain most often repeated during his journey from birth to death.

Mohammed's death plunged the new Moslem nation into confusion and uncertainty. His followers refused to believe that the Prophet had been mortal until Abu Bakr, his closest friend, reminded them that, unlike Christians who worshiped Christ, there were no such thing as Mohammedans. Moslems must worship only Allah, not the Messenger of Allah.

Mohammed had left no male heir, nor had he clearly indicated his own choice to succeed him. Old tribal feuds broke out anew in the struggle for Moslem leadership. An assembly of sheikhs finally chose Abu Bakr, who was also a father-in-law of the Prophet, as Commander of the Faithful. Followers of Ali, Mohammed's cousin and son-in-law, were incensed.

Within a few years the Moslem world was split by a schism as deep as that which divided Jews and Christians, Roman Catholics and the Greek Orthodox Church, or Catholics and Protestants. The Umayyads who ruled Mecca formed the supporters of Abu Bakr into the Sunnis, while those who insisted Ali was the rightful successor became the rival Shias.

Despite their feud, the Moslem armies Mohammed had built remained united and strong. Under Abu Bakr and his successor as caliph, Omar, these fierce Bedouin warriors swept out of the desert to conquer Syria, Persia, Jerusalem, and Egypt in just six years, from 636 to 642. The watching world was astonished at the speed with which these nations fell under the sword of Islam. Religious indoctrination by the Koran followed, along with the spread of the Arabic language.

In 661 transfer of the Moslem caliphate to the Syrian capital of Damascus marked the founding of the Umayyad Dynasty that lasted almost a century. The Umayyads stretched Islamic power all the way across North Africa to Spain, and across the Middle East to India, the largest empire in world history.

Under their rule many Jewish and Christian administrators were relied upon to manage the complexities of daily affairs of state, while the caliph and his viziers devoted themselves to wars, propagation of the faith, and the enjoyment of power.

Arab expansion received its first military check in 732, when the Umayyads were repulsed in France by the Battle of Poitiers, marking a turning point for the Arab Empire. Fifteen years later the rule of the Umayyads was overthrown by the Abbasids, with the aid of Persian converts. The seat of Islamic power was transferred to Baghdad, a magnificent new circular city in Iraq built by one hundred thousand craftsmen from all over the empire.

The caliphate now became less of an Arab sheikhdom than a Persian despotism, with Persian ideas, art forms, literature, and science supplanting the more primitive culture of the Arabian desert. The five-hundred-year sophisticated rule of the Abbasids was a far cry from Mohammed's austere concept of a Moslem empire. No longer sheikhs ruling by tribal consent, the caliphs now claimed to rule by "divine will." Frequent use of court executioners discouraged disagreement.

Baghdad became an exotic world market center with ships sailing up to its wharves carrying silks, spices, and jewels from China, India, Ceylon, and East Africa, as well as slaves taken in war. Arab sea merchants — immortalized by Sinbad the Sailor in *The Arabian Nights* — carried foodstuffs, linen, perfumes, pearls, and handicrafts from Baghdad to the Orient and Europe.

The most famous Abbasid caliph was the half-Persian Harun al-Rashid, who ruled from 763 to 809. It was he who began what became known as the Golden Age of the Arab Empire, renowned for the magnificence of his court and the arts he patronized. The world of Harun, portrayed in all its splendor and glory in *The Arabian Nights,* has vanished, but not its power to enthrall and delight the Arab mind.

Harun's court attracted poets, wits, musicians, singers, dancers, artists, and all who could add color and charm to the luxury-loving caliph's days. He was so moved by the beauty of song that one slave wrote and sang, that he instantly freed the singer and poured a hundred thousand dinars into his lap.

Women vied with men in composing poetry, and brightened the court with their wit, songs, and musical talent. In this early period of the Abbasids, highborn women often exercised influence in affairs of state, and were even allowed to seek distinction on the field of battle.

From tent dwellers and desert riders, the Arabs became patrons of the architectural arts, with skilled engineers, craftsmen, and artists conscripted from all over the empire to design, construct, and decorate beautiful mosques and other buildings. The ornamental style known as arabesque used interlaced vines, plants, and flowers as inspiration for abstract designs.

Arab artists developed calligraphy — handwriting perfected as fine art. Just as Christian monks of the Middle Ages often spent their lives writing and illuminating religious manuscripts, many Abbasid artists devoted their lives to producing beautifully handcrafted copies of the Koran. Calligraphy also played tricks with words, transforming them into birds, flowers, and other images, pleasing eye and mind simultaneously.

Everything that Harun did was on the grand scale. When the Byzantines sent their envoys to Baghdad, he greeted them with seven hundred chamberlains, seven thousand eunuchs, one hundred sixty thousand cavalrymen and foot soldiers, and a parade of a hundred lions. His palace was decorated with gilt curtains and twenty-two thousand rugs, while mechanical birds sang metallic songs in a tree made of gold and silver.

A pious believer, Harun gave bountifully to the poor, and built rest lodges all along the route of the pilgrimage to Mecca. But he was merciless to his enemies. Leading his army on an expedition to suppress a rebellion in Samarkand, he fell gravely ill just as the rebel leader's brother was captured.

Asked what should be done with the prisoner, Harun replied, "If I had no more breath left but for two words, they would be — slay him." On that note he died in 809.

Under his son Mamun, an army of well-paid scholars were put to work at a House of Knowledge, translating philosophical, scientific and literary manuscripts from Greek, Syrian, Persian, and Sanskrit into Arabic. A reawakening Europe fed on this source of wisdom when Plato, Aristotle, and Galen's important medical text, *Anatomy,* were retranslated from Arabic into Latin.

The Abassids also developed the sciences of geography and astronomy, understandable pursuits for sea-roving merchants and desert travelers who navigated by the stars. Fixing the stars was also helpful in locating the direction of Mecca for prayer. An astronomical laboratory was set up to plot the orbits of the planets. Mamun's geographers accurately measured the size of the earth, and insisted many hundreds of years before Columbus that it was round. They also produced a great atlas of the world, with the history of each country.

Arab mathemeticians, borrowing Hindu methods of calculation, developed Arabic numerals and algebra, replacing the clumsy Roman numerals that made the simplest calculations difficult. Once principally a language of poetry and religious revelation, under Mamun Arabic also became the preeminent language of science and philosophy.

Intellectual brilliance flourished to the point that Abbasid scholars often excelled in a number of different disciplines outside their specialties. Thus many translators were also physicians and mathematicians; physicians were also philosophers and musicians. The poet Omar Khayyam, famous for his poem the *Rubaiyat,* was also a distinguished astronomer.

What made the Golden Age of the Arab Empire glitter even more remarkably in history was that it created a great center of civilization while Europe was still in the Dark Ages.

"Arab scholars were studying Aristotle when Charlemagne and his lords were reportedly learning to write their names," observed Princeton historian Philip K. Hitti. "Scientists in Cordova, with their seventeen great libraries, one alone of which included more than 400,000 volumes, enjoyed luxurious baths at a time when washing the body was considered a dangerous custom at the University of Oxford."

Arab intellectuals expressed contempt for "the peoples of the north," considering them to suffer from chilled bodies and brains, and in Arab eyes, the Vikings were simply barbarians. "The warm humor is lacking among them," observed a tenth-century geographer, Masudi. "Their bodies are large, their natures gross, their manners harsh, their understanding dull and their tongues heavy . . . their religious beliefs lack solidity . . . those of them who are farthest to the north are the most subject to stupidity, grossness and brutishness."

No Western country was so deeply affected by the Arabs as Spain, where the Moslem occupation lasted almost eight hundred years. Spain's heritage in art, architecture, music, science, and philosophy is heavily Arabic. Today Arabs and Spaniards still share over four thousand Arabic words in common. Bells peal in Catholic church towers that were built as Moslem minarets. Heavy iron door knockers shaped as hands symbolize the hand of Fatima, the daughter of Mohammed.

European medical knowledge was largely derived from Arabic medical books translated into Latin. Even by the fourteenth century, plague was considered an "act of God" in Christian Europe, while Moslem physicians in Spain had already proved that it was a contagious disease. The Arabs also established the first drugstores and the first school of pharmacy.

"The torch of Islamic learning . . . lit the lamps of Europe's medieval scholars," declared Dr. Seyyed Hossain Nasr, Harvard-educated historian.

After Mamun's death, the caliphate fell under Turkish influence and became a sultanate. Under a sultan who was little more than a ceremonial figure, captured Turks called Mamelukes won control of the empire's armed forces. The empire began to fall apart as military commanders and political adventurers struggled against each other for power.

Egypt fell into the hands of a Shia sect, the Fatimids, who extended their power into Palestine, Syria, North Africa, Sicily, and western Arabia. For a while they were more influential in the Arab world than the sultanate at Baghdad.

The Umayyad caliphate of Spain fell in 1031, splintering into twenty different petty dynasties and republics, each falling prey to a Christian king of Europe.

One of the strangest Arab princedoms was Alamut, a mountain fortress in northern Persia ruled by Hassan ibn-al-Sabbah, who organized a systematic program of assassination against Syrian leaders. Bands of devoted youth, trained to fanatical obedience, were taught the techniques of murder by poison, dagger, garrote, and bare hands. Marco Polo wrote about Hassan, referring to him as "the Old Man of the Mountains."

Next to his palace Hassan maintained a harem of beautiful girls in a lovely pavilion with perfumed gardens. As part of their training, the young assassins were heavily drugged with hashish (marijuana) and wine, then woke to find themselves in the gardens, each with a coterie of beauties at his command. After several days of such rapture they were again drugged and transferred to a palace room before Hassan.

He explained to the dazed youths that they had been given a glimpse of Paradise, where they would spend their afterlife as a reward for carrying out Hassan's suicidal missions of assassination. If they were killed in the attempt, he assured them, they would only return to Paradise sooner.

Hassan's reign of terror won him control of most of Syria. His followers were called Assassins, possibly after the hashish (*hashishi*) with which he drugged them, and became associated with the politics of murder, not unlike today's political terrorists. Eventually the Assassins disappeared as a sect when they were massacred by Mongol invaders.

In 1095, when the Moslems threatened to take Constantinople, the Byzantine Emperor Alexius Comnenus appealed to Pope Urban II for help, suggesting that the Greek Church and Rome unite behind the Cross to defeat the Crescent. The Pope agreed and issued a call for a crusade against "the wicked race."

Most of the Crusaders were activated less by spiritual motives than by boredom, the desire for adventure, and a lust for booty. Some leaders hoped to seize and rule fiefdoms. Criminals were given their release to enlist; the poor and hungry joined for food. The Crusades descended upon the Middle East in nine waves over the next two centuries.

On June 7, 1099, Crusaders broke into Jerusalem and massacred Arabs and Jews mercilessly, sparing neither women nor children. Jews who took refuge in the chief synagogue were burned alive. Plundering the city and taking over homes, the Crusaders celebrated a "holy victory against the infidels."

The Arab Empire had fallen into such decay and disunity that the Moslems were unable to close ranks against the invaders. "How long will Arab heroes endure such injury," wailed poet Abi-wardi, "and submit to disgrace from the barbarians?"

Not until 1187 were the Arabs again united enough to seriously challenge the Crusaders in Palestine. The leader who united them was Saladin, who had overthrown the Fatimid dynasty of Egypt. Assembling a great Arab army, he defeated the Crusaders in a major battle at Tiberias. Much more humane than his Christian enemies, he permitted none in Palestine to be harmed, and allowed most prisoners to be ransomed.

The victory put all of Syria and most of Palestine in Saladin's hands, and threatened the last outpost of the Crusaders. These outposts were reinforced by a third Crusade led by England's King Richard the Lion Hearted, who placed Jerusalem under a mighty siege. Building street barricades, Saladin set an example for both rich and poor by carrying stones on his own shoulders.

He succeeded in holding off the Crusaders, but was compelled to sign a treaty giving Christian pilgrims the right to visit Jerusalem to hold services. King Richard, ignoring Saladin's merciful example, beheaded over two thousand Arab prisoners.

Saladin proved as enlightened a ruler as he was a skilled and generous general. He encouraged scholarship, founded schools and mosques, dug irrigation canals and built dikes. When he died in 1192, he was mourned by the Arabs as the savior of Palestine, who had also bound Egypt, Syria, and Iraq into one empire.

In 1212 a fifth Crusade organized three armies of children in France and Germany, led by a young shepherd known as Stephen of Cloyes. They were offered passage to the Holy Land by two Marseilles merchants, who turned out to be slave dealers with secret arrangements to provide young slaves for wealthy Moslems. After sailing, the young pilgrims of the Children's Crusade were not heard of again for eighteen years.

A priest who had accompanied them finally managed to return to Europe to tell their grim story. Most had died in slavery in Alexandria. The children who had followed Stephen of Cloyes to their dismal fate were the source of the famous folktale of the Pied Piper of Hamelin.

While the Arabs continued to fight off the Crusades the Pope threw against them, a new enemy arose in the east. The huge Mongol armies of Genghis Khan were sweeping over China, Korea, Russia, and Syria. In 1258 they captured Baghdad. Killing the last Abbasid caliph in a general massacre, the Mongols abolished the caliphate and sacked the city.

The fall of Baghdad marked the formal end of the once tremendously successful Arab Empire. Rule of the Moslem world was transferred to barbarian hands except for Egypt and Palestine, successfully defended by the armies of Baybars, a former Mameluke slave who had made himself sultan of Egypt.

The tattered Islamic heritage now fell back to the outpost of Cairo, which became its standard-bearer. Arab culture continued to flourish here and in Spain for two more centuries, as Baybars also hurled back the last of the Crusaders. No Saladin, Baybars slaughtered sixteen thousand Christians at Antioch, and sold a hundred thousand Christian men, women, and children into slavery.

Despite ruin at the hands of the Mongols, Arab hatred was greater for the arrogant Crusaders who, for two centuries, had brought the Arab Empire low by siege, slaughter, and pillage. The Crusaders left a legacy of Arab bitterness that laid the basis for a hostility toward, and suspicion of, the West that persists to the present day.

Ironically, the Mongols who conquered the Moslem world were in turn conquered spiritually by Islam. One of the fruits of their conversion was the Sufi movement, a Sunni sect that emphasizes individual worship rather than ritualism.

The defeated Crusaders, who had set out for the Middle East scornful of the "ignorant infidels," returned home respectful of the refinements of Moslem civilization they had found. As a result, Europeans were introduced to public baths, a carrier-pigeon postal service, percussion instruments, the navigational compass, and Arabian literature, spices, perfumes, fabrics, sugar, and candy.

Western science also progressed rapidly during the twelfth and thirteenth centuries, thanks to Latin translations of the Arabic books of Greek and Byzantine knowledge.

Disillusioned by the decline of the once-powerful Arab Empire, a great Arab scholar, Ibn Khaldun (1332–1406), urged his people to return to the old desert ways. The best government, he wrote, was the one that governed least and let every man rely upon himself for his own needs.

"Look at all the countries that the Arabs have dominated and subjugated from the beginning of things," he pointed out. "Their civilization has been decimated, their inhabitants impoverished." He called for a renunciation of Sybaritic luxuries, such as those introduced by the Abbasids, as artificial and corrupting; Arabs were meant for the desert life.

The Tartar hordes of another barbarian, Tamerlane, ravished Syria and Iraq between 1393 and 1404, defeating both the Egyptian and Turkish armies. Sacking Baghdad and burning Damascus, Tamerlane built horrendous towers of skulls to commemorate his victories. He dealt a further blow to Middle East civilization by carrying off the most learned scholars and artisans to his capital in Central Asia.

One Arab scholar traveled even farther when he sailed as interpreter on the *Santa Maria,* in the same year the Christians completed their conquest of Spain. Quickly converting to Christianity out of fear of persecution and changing his name to Louis De Torres, he became the first Arab to set foot in America. Columbus had been greatly influenced by the Arab sciences spreading from Spain, particularly by Arab insistence that a "new world" existed beyond the "sea of darkness."

When the Cross supplanted the Crescent in Spain, the Christian rulers showed Moslems and Jews none of the tolerance Christians and Jews had normally found under Islam. Arabic books were hurled into bonfires, destroying priceless knowledge, and an Inquisition tortured or deported stubborn infidels.

Final humiliation of the Arabs came between 1515 and 1517 when the army of Ottoman Turks swept into Syria, Iraq, and Egypt. Ottoman Sultan Selim I, who had captured Constantinople, became master of the Arab world. The Sherif of Mecca meekly presented him with the keys of the Holy City, and awarded him the title of Protector of the Holy Places.

For the next four centuries of rule by thirty-six Ottoman sultans, Arabs everywhere were compelled to pray to Allah to bless the Turkish rulers who had conquered them.

# 6

# Under Despotism and Colonialism

THUS BEGAN modern Arab history. Ruling from Constantinople, the Ottoman sultans controlled their empire through Turkish viceroys called pashas, who were stationed in each provincial capital with a force of Janissary troops. The greater the distance between a pasha and the "Sublime Porte," the more autonomy he enjoyed, as a rule, as long as he diligently collected and paid taxes to Constantinople.

Outright Turkish rule was a bitter pill for the Arabs to swallow, particularly since their subjection came at the hands of fellow Moslems they themselves had converted. Powerless in the lands they had once ruled, Arab men were subject to conscription, beating, and abuse by the harsh Janissaries.

Their wounded pride often led them to salve their battered egos by tyrannical behavior toward their families. Women lost many of the rights and the status they had once enjoyed under the Arab Empire. Their husbands and fathers emulated the Turks in veiling them and restricting them severely to the home. The Arab male's lack of freedom outside the home led to the female's lack of freedom within it.

In 1609 Philip III of Spain ordered all Moslems left on Spanish soil to either convert to Christianity or face mass deportation. Since there was no purely Arab state left to return to, about half a million were forced to sail to Morocco, the one Barbary Coast country not under Turkish rule.

Some who made this choice had reason to regret it when mad Moulay Ismail became sultan of Morocco. Whenever he wore yellow, his "killing color," he would mount his horse and strike off the heads of everyone within reach with his scimitar. Kicking and beating slaves, he also burned and impaled them for sport.

Arab pride and nationalism remained crushed until a wandering merchant in Arabia, Mohammed ibn Abdul Wahab (1703–1787), sought to revive Arab unity and power with a movement based on Ibn Khaldun's cry for a return to the puritanical Islam of the desert. Prince Mohammed Ibn Saud put an army behind the Wahabis, who unified many feuding tribes of Arabia.

Raiding Syria, Iraq, and other parts of the former Arab Empire with the cry "Back to the Koran!," the Wahabi rising stirred fresh hope among Arabs throughout the Ottoman Empire. Revolts broke out in Egypt and Syria.

The Turks were less worried about the Wahabis, however, than about an aggressive Europe driven by commercial rivalry. At the end of the eighteenth century both England and France viewed Egypt as the door to European control of India. In 1798 an army under Napoleon landed in Egypt, ostensibly to overthrow the Mamelukes on behalf of the Ottoman sultan, in reality to gain a French base for invading India and the Far East.

"People of Egypt," Napoleon said, "you are told that I come to destroy your religion. Do not believe it. Reply that I come to restore your rights, punish the usurpers, and that I respect, more than the Mamelukes, God, His Prophet and the Koran." But later he confessed, "I was full of dreams. I saw myself founding a religion, marching into Asia, riding an elephant, a turban on my head and in my hand the new Koran that I would have composed to suit my needs."

Not deceived by Napoleon, the Porte set about raising armies from all parts of the empire, calling on "all true believers to take arms against those swinish infidels, the French." The sultan allied himself with France's traditional foe, the British, in driving the French out of Egypt.

A fierce, ambitious Turkish officer named Mohammed Ali distinguished himself in the campaign, and was made pasha of Egypt in 1805. He swept aside Mameluke resistance by massacring two dozen of their princes, subdued the rival Wahabis in Arabia, and also conquered Sudan, Palestine, Lebanon, and Syria. When he sought to capture Constantinople itself, he was sternly warned off by the Porte's ally, England.

Mohammed Ali proved one of the more enlightened pashas. He destroyed Egypt's feudal class by confiscating their lands and renting them directly to the fellahin for taxes. In 1821 he introduced the cultivation of cotton, using new scientific methods of agriculture, and founded Egypt's first schools of engineering and modern medicine. He also arranged the first cultural exchange of Arab scholars with Europe.

His son Ibrahim was given Syria to rule. In 1823 Ibrahim encouraged European and American missionaries to set up their own schools in the Middle East. This led to the establishment of what is now the renowned American University of Beirut.

European pressure compelled the Porte to sign a commercial

code in 1838 that threw open all of the Middle East to European merchants, giving them great trading advantages over Arab competitors. They were also granted "capitulations," which acknowledged the right of the merchants to follow their own customs and laws while in the Middle East, making them untouchable by Moslem courts. Immunity to punishment led the Europeans to commit flagrant abuses against the Arabs.

Europeans increasingly found it safe to tour the volatile Middle East, among them French novelist Gustave Flaubert and a companion, Maxime du Camp. They were fascinated by the differences between Western and Arab society. In 1849 they attended a religious ceremony that reenacted the legend of a Moslem saint who reputedly had ridden his horse into Cairo over clay jars, without breaking any. The saint was impersonated by a sheikh who rode his mount over the backs of two hundred men, lying prone side by side to simulate the jars.

"If the men die," Flaubert noted wryly, "it is due to their sins." He added that to drive back the crowds, "a veritable tornado of bastinados [beatings] was rained right and left by the eunuchs on anyone who happened to be within reach."

The Arab population, he found, manifested little interest in any change of rulers. "Under different names it will always remain the same," Flaubert wrote, "and will gain nothing because it has nothing to lose."

Du Camp saw groaning Arab shopkeepers who had been nailed by their ears to a wheat storehouse, with only their toes touching the ground, for cheating on the weight or quality of goods sold. Far from disapproving, he wrote, "This is an excellent measure that we would do well to borrow from the Orientals; their ways are sometimes wiser than ours."

Westernization began overtaking Egypt in 1854 when a concession to build the Suez Canal was granted to French promoter Ferdinand de Lesseps. The French-educated khedive of Egypt,

Ismail, accepted huge loans offered by European banks to develop the canal, and to build rail lines, harbor works, bridges, a telegraph system, and primary schools. He also introduced a parliament in 1866, the first Mideast vestige of democracy.

By 1875 he was so deeply in debt to the banks that he was compelled to sell Egypt's interest in the Suez Canal to the British government. Britain lost no time in using this foothold to gain control of and exploit Egyptian resources.

Arab nationalists, disguised as a Syrian scientific society with headquarters in Beirut, began secretly posting placards exhorting Arabs to rise against the Ottoman Empire. The Turks were denounced for attempting to suppress the Arabic tongue, usurping the caliphate, and breaking the laws of Islam.

Each morning, as crowds collected around the posters, police would rush to rip them down and arrest suspects.

Sultan Abd al-Hamid used over thirty thousand spies and *agents provocateurs* to ferret out troublemakers, and censored all publications. To keep Arabs too busy fighting each other to unite against Constantinople, he provoked intertribal feuds. His tactics managed to frustrate the hopes of Arab nationalists for the thirty-two years of his reign.

In 1879 the British compelled Egypt's Khedive Ismael to step down in favor of his son Tewfik, who could be more easily manipulated as a puppet for British commercial interests. Two years later an army colonel, Arabi Pasha, led a revolt. British forces crushed it, occupied Cairo, and stayed on in open control for another seventy-four years on the pretext of being needed to manage Egypt's bankrupt economy.

Arab nationalists accused the British of exploiting Egypt for the benefit of their textile magnates, who needed fine Egyptian cotton for the mills of Lancashire. The British occupation was also intended to protect their route to India through the Suez, the traffic of which was eighty percent British.

They also took control of Sudan to the south, where Mohammed Ahmed, an obscure Arab fakir who called himself the Mahdi (Expected One), began a *jihad* to drive all foreigners out. In 1883 a dervish army led by the Mahdi inflicted a decisive defeat on a ten-thousand-man Egyptian army led by the British.

A popular British war hero, General Charles Gordon, was rushed to Khartoum to save the situation. Refusing to lead a retreat or to surrender when a five-month siege made his position hopeless, he was killed as the Mahdi's forces took Khartoum. British General Herbert Kitchener avenged his death in 1898 by smashing the Sudanese army and capturing the Mahdi's successor, who was whipped in chains through the streets.

By 1908 a revolutionary movement against the Ottoman Empire had made such headway that sultan Abdul-Hamid feared for his throne. The opposition came not only from Arab nationalists but also from disgruntled Turkish army officers known as the Young Turks. The sultan sought to forestall rebellion by releasing all political prisoners, adopting a constitution, ending censorship, and abolishing his thirty-thousand-spy army.

Gaining political power under the new constitutional regime, the Young Turks saw no reason to share it with the Arab nationalists. They banned all non-Turkish societies and imposed stricter control over all Arab provinces. Arab nationalists were forced to revive their own secret resistance groups.

Taking advantage of a weakened Ottoman Empire, European powers began seizing Arab territory. In 1911 the Italians took Libya. In 1912 the French, who already controlled Algeria and Tunisia, made Morocco a protectorate. These new invasions provoked furious Arab demonstrations in Alexandria.

At a 1913 Arab congress in Beirut, nationalists demanded that the Porte stop these power grabs, grant home rule to all Arab provinces, let Arab schools teach in Arabic, and end conscription of Arabs to serve outside their own countries. When the Turks turned a deaf ear, Arab nationalists began plotting to make a secret deal with a major European power to help overthrow the Ottoman Empire.

The opportunity came when Europe went to war in August 1914, with Turkey joining Germany against Britain, France, Italy, and Russia. The sultan issued a call to all Moslems for Holy War against the Allies. To make it binding, however, it had to be endorsed by the grand sherif of Mecca, Hussein ibn Ali, descendant of the Prophet and custodian of the Holy Places.

Stalling the Porte on a public call for *jihad,* Hussein sent his son Abdullah from Mecca to Cairo, to negotiate secretly with the British high commissioner, Sir Henry McMahon. They reached an accord by which Hussein agreed to organize a revolt against the Turks, in return for which, after the war, the British would recognize Hussein as caliph of an independent Arab nation whose exact boundaries would be determined later.

But soon afterward, unknown to Hussein, the British made contradictory commitments in secret negotiations with France. In the spring of 1916 Sir Mark Sykes and F. Georges Picot concluded an agreement to divide the Middle East into spheres of influence that ignored the McMahon-Hussein accord. No provision whatever was made for any independent Arab state. Worse, Arab boundaries were redrawn so as to split apart nationalities, scrambling populations deliberately so that disunity within each Arab country would be assured.

Kept in the dark about the Sykes-Picot accord, Hussein passed the word to the Arab secret societies to begin organizing a revolt. Informed by spies, Jemal Pasha, Syria's brutal governor-general, arrested twenty-one leading citizens of Damascus and Beirut who may or may not have been involved, tried them for treason, and hanged them on May 6, 1916. It was a fatal blunder. Total revulsion for the Turks swept the Arab world.

On June 6 Sherif Hussein publicly proclaimed the Arab revolt, crying, "Death has become sweet, O Arabs!" With that battle cry his forces attacked the Turkish garrison in Mecca, aided by Egyptian artillery companies sent by the British. They captured the city on July 9, and an independent Arab state was proclaimed with the sherif as its king.

"Unfortunately," Jemal Pasha declared bitterly, "the holy *jihad* has been blocked by a mean individual, who, in the very heart of the Holy Land of Islam, has allied himself to those Christian Powers whose object it is to despoil the world of Islam and purloin Constantinople, its capital. That vile individual, who is not ashamed to call himself a descendant of the Prophet . . . has compelled the Ottoman Empire to dispatch forces against him, which should have been defeating the British." Jemal vowed to cut off the head of "that scoundrel in Mecca."

In October 1916 the British dispatched a young intelligence officer, Thomas Edward Lawrence, to the Hejaz to serve as military advisor to the army of Hussein's son Feisal. Lawrence of Arabia, as he was to become known, was an enigmatic archeologist and engineer who knew the Arab people well and spoke their language.

At Feisal's side, Lawrence raided Turkish railways, demolishing tracks, bridges, and culverts, and inflicting other hit-and-run blows against the enemy. His raids were timed to do the most damage to the Turks in coordination with British-led Egyptian forces. Feisal's raiders drove into Syria and the Sinai peninsula in a series of stunning and unexpected victories against much larger Turkish armies.

A colorful figure, Lawrence commanded the respect of the Bedouin in billowing robes he rode with, keeping the curved daggers of the various tribes turned away from each other. "My men were bloodthirsty enemies of thirty tribes," he wrote later in his reminiscences, *Revolt in the Desert,* "and only for my hand over them would have murdered in the ranks each day. Their feuds prevented them combining against me."

He admired three traits among the illiterate sheikhs, however — their passionate dedication to Arab freedom, their reverence for Arab history, and their love of the Arabic language. The Arabs, in turn, admired Lawrence as a brilliant military tactician, but tended to resent the impression given the world that he alone was responsible for Arab victories.

Hussein's son Abdullah called Lawrence "the uncrowned king of the Arabs," but wrote: "He was certainly a strange character. His intrigues went as far as an attempt to influence me against my own father on the pretext that my father was obstinate."

Lawrence's postwar books about his desert experiences enjoyed great popularity. Through their prism, the West gained a new understanding of Arab culture and thought, and of the Arab struggle for independence, equality, and world respect after centuries of humiliation by the non-Arab world.

But the Lawrence cult, which began by celebrating the Arabs as brave, dignified, proud Bedouin fighters, soon degenerated into sentimental romanticism, vulgarized by movies like *The Sheik of Araby* with Rudolph Valentino. This and other parodies of desert life grotesquely distorted the Arab image, which had to wait over forty years for correction by a film like *Lawrence of Arabia*.

During World War I, Dr. Chaim Weizmann, a Russian-born Jewish chemist in England, developed a substitute process for making TNT when the British were desperately short of acetone. Asked to name his reward, Weizmann was interested only in aiding the Zionist cause he led, dedicated to creating a "home in Palestine for those Jews who cannot or will not be assimilated by the country of their adoption."

Weizmann assured British Foreign Secretary Lord Arthur Balfour that the Zionists had no wish to control the Holy Places of Jerusalem, nor to set up a Jewish republic, nor to gain any special rights not enjoyed by other Palestinians.

On November 2, 1917, Balfour issued the famous Balfour Declaration, after winning approval for it from American President Woodrow Wilson and the French government. It declared, "His Majesty's Government view with favour the establishment of a National Home for the Jewish People, and will use their best endeavors to facilitate the achievement of this object, it being clearly understood that nothing shall be done which may prejudice the civil and religious rights of existing non-Jewish communities in Palestine, or the rights and political status enjoyed by Jews in any other country."

This carefully worded but deliberately vague document became the Magna Carta for the state of Israel, and the cause of furious dispute, not only in the Middle East, but also in the United Nations and between the world's superpowers, provoking endless wars and worldwide terrorism.

In the Arabian desert Prince Abdullah told Lawrence angrily, "As for the people of Palestine, they refuse the Balfour Declaration and insist on the retention of the Arab character of Palestine. We shall not agree to the annihilation of the Arabs for the sake of the Jews. The Arabs are not like trees which, when cut, grow again."

At the time of the declaration, less than five percent of the population of Palestine were native Jews. Sir Harold Nicholson, who participated in the drafting, said later, "We believed that we were founding a refuge for the disabled, and did not foresee that it would become a nest of hornets."

An outraged Hussein demanded an explanation from the British for the violation of the McMahon-Hussein accord. He was reassured by the British Arab Bureau in Cairo that Jewish settlement in Palestine would be allowed only "insofar as it was consistent with the freedom of the existing population, both economic and political."

When Weizmann visited the Mideast at the head of a Zionist delegation, he promised Feisal that the Zionists would not attempt to establish a Jewish government in Palestine, wishing only to create a Jewish refuge from European persecution. The Zionists, Weizmann assured him, intended to cooperate in building an independent Arab state of Palestine.

In December 1917, following the Russian Revolution, a copy of the secret Sykes-Picot accord was found in czarist archives by Soviet leaders. During German-Russian truce negotiations, Trotsky showed it to the Germans, who showed it to Jemal Pasha in Syria. Jemal sent a copy to Feisal, pointing out that his father had been tricked into supporting the British in the war by false promises of Arab independence. The secret Sykes-Picot accord clearly proved that Britain had no intention of keeping these promises. Jemal offered the Arabs a separate peace granting their provinces full autonomy under the Ottoman Empire.

The Arabs were stunned by this evidence of the perfidy of colonialism. Coming on top of the Balfour Declaration, it convinced many Arab nationalists that they could no longer trust Great Britain. Others, however, were even less willing to trust the Turks. Hussein angrily demanded that the London government reaffirm its pledges to the Arabs publicly.

In June 1918, fearful of an Arab withdrawal from the war, the British announced they would "recognize the complete and sovereign independence of the Arabs . . . and support them in their struggle for freedom . . . based on the problem of the consent of the governed." General Edmund Allenby, British high commissioner in Egypt, urged Feisal to place his trust wholeheartedly in the just intentions of the Allies.

These assurances, plus President Wilson's Fourteen Points

speech in July, persuaded the principal Arab leaders that all postwar settlements would be based on people's self-determination.

As the war moved toward a climax, Feisal sought to speed his army to Damascus ahead of the British and French forces, hoping by capturing the capital of Syria to strengthen the Arab claim to it. He won the race by a few days on October 1, 1918, and in fierce fighting drove the Turks out.

Arab patriots in Damascus staged a joyful celebration. When the Arab flag was raised two days later in Beirut, however, the French protested indignantly and Allenby ordered it taken down. The news almost provoked a mutiny among Feisal's forces in Damascus. He warned Allenby that he could no longer control the Arab army without an unequivocal Allied declaration of Arab rights. The British compelled the French to join in a new proclamation supporting the principle of postwar rule of all Arab lands only by the consent of the governed.

The Ottoman Empire surrendered four weeks after the capture of Damascus, ending four centuries of tyrannical rule over the Arabs. The war ended with the British in control of all Arab forces, and French bureaucrats ruling their Arab territories through puppet pashas. Neither power had any intention of relinquishing its spoils, although Sir Mark Sykes now regretted his role in betraying British promises to the Arabs. He sought to make amends by convincing the Versailles Peace Conference that the Arabs were entitled to their independence, but died while the diplomats were still deliberating.

Hussein sent Feisal to London to demand fulfillment of the Allies' promises. Lawrence pleaded the Arabs' cause with the British government, but was told that Feisal could best speed independence by accepting the Balfour Declaration. Pressured by Lawrence, on January 3, 1919, Feisal signed an accord with Weizmann agreeing to Zionist emigration to Palestine. Recognizing the "national aspirations" of both Jews and Arabs, it permitted large-scale Jewish immigration provided "Arab peasant and tenant farmers would be protected in their rights."

Feisal carefully added a proviso that would nullify the agreement if the Versailles conference failed to grant Arab independence within the borders demanded by his father.

He looked to the Zionists for aid in building an Arab state of Palestine. At a Zionist dinner given by Lord Rothschild, Feisal declared, "Dr. Weizmann's ideals are ours, and we will expect you, without our asking, to help us in return. No state can be built up in the Near East without the goodwill of the Great Powers, but it requires more than that. It requires the borrowing from Europe of ideals and materials and knowledge and experience. To make these fit for us, we must translate them from European shape to Arab shape — and what intermediary could we find in the world more suitable than you? For you have all the knowledge of Europe and are cousins by blood."

But Feisal had underestimated Arab opposition to the Balfour Declaration which Lawrence had persuaded him to endorse. In a stormy session at an Arab congress in Damascus, his agreement with Weizmann was repudiated. Feisal was forced to advise the Zionists that only limited Jewish immigration to Palestine could be allowed, and that any Jewish homeland could only be a province within a larger Arab state.

After promising to send a commission of inquiry to the Middle East to sound out public opinion on what form of government Arabs wanted, Britain and France reneged. But Wilson, who had promised self-determination for all peoples as an Allied war aim, sent two American commissioners in the summer of 1919.

After six weeks in Palestine and Syria they submitted the King-Crane report, a confidential study for Wilson not made public for another three years. The Arabs, reported the commissioners, were demanding independence for Syria, including Palestine as a sovereign state, under Feisal as king; recognition of Iraqi independence; and repudiation of both the Sykes-Picot accord and the Balfour Declaration.

The King-Crane report recommended that the Arab states be prepared for independence as American or British mandates. It cautioned the Allies that the Arabs were fiercely opposed to either Zionist penetration of Palestine or French penetration of Syria. The commissioners also noted that Zionist representatives were planning to take over Palestine as a Jewish state by buying out most of the Arabs who lived in it.

"The extreme Zionist Program must be greatly modified," they warned. "For 'a national home for the Jewish people' is not equivalent to making Palestine into a Jewish State; nor can the erection of such a Jewish State be accomplished without the gravest trespass upon the 'civil and religious rights of existing non-Jewish communities in Palestine.' . . . The initial claim, often submitted by Zionist representatives, that they have a 'right' to Palestine, based on an occupation of two thousand years ago, can hardly be seriously considered."

The peacemakers at Versailles ignored the warning.

On August 11, 1919, in a secret memo to the British Foreign Office, Balfour admitted that Allied duplicity toward the Arabs was the result of a deliberate policy of deception.

"France, England and America have got themselves into a position over the Syrian problem so inextricably confused," he wrote, "that no really neat and satisfactory issue is now possible. . . . The four Great Powers are committed to Zionism. And Zionism, be it right or wrong, good or bad, is rooted in age-long traditions, in present needs, in future hopes, of far profounder import than the desires and prejudices of the 700,000 Arabs who now inhabit that ancient land. . . . The Powers . . . do not propose to consult them. . . . The Powers have made no statement of fact which is not admittedly wrong, and no declaration of policy . . . they have not always intended to violate."

The British Foreign Office agreed with Balfour's position that if the British had to quarrel with someone over the problem, it had better be with the powerless Arabs than with the powerful French. So when British troops pulled out of Syria and Lebanon, they turned over key coastal positions to French forces. Feisal even found his own army being taken over by Arab officers who had been pro-Turk.

At that point, betrayed by the British he had trusted to keep their word, Feisal repudiated his understanding with the Zionists, since his conditions for validating the Balfour Declaration had been violated. In March 1920 an Arab national congress declared Syria, Lebanon, and Palestine independent, a constitutional monarchy under Feisal as king. A similar congress in Iraq proclaimed that country also independent, with Feisal's brother Abdullah as king.

One month later England and France gave their reply at the San Remo Conference. Contemptuously ignoring Arab declarations of independence, they carved the borders of the Middle East into the Arab nations that we know today, placing all of them under mandatory rule. Syria was broken up into three countries — Palestine, Lebanon, and a smaller Syria. Syria and Lebanon were to become French mandates. Britain was to be the mandate power for Iraq and Palestine.

Arab sovereignty was permitted only in the Arabian Peninsula, which was considered too inhospitable as well as too unprofitable to annex. It was split up into five independent states, the two most important being the Hejaz under King Hussein and Najd under King Ibn Saud, whose fierce rivalry with Hussein could be counted on to prevent Arab unity.

There was fresh dismay in the Arab camp when an important British Zionist, Sir Herbert Samuel, was named high commissioner of Palestine. That news, on top of the decisions at San Remo, swept away any last illusions Arab nationalists may have held about the wisdom of trusting the Great Powers.

In the Arab world 1920 became infamous as the Year of Calamity — the year Arab hopes turned to ashes.

# 7

## The Arabs
## and the Jews

THE ZIONISTS laid claim to Palestine on the basis of the Jewish conquest of the land in the days of Joshua and King David, and because in Genesis God is quoted as saying to Abraham, "Unto thy seed will I give this land." Rejecting their claim, the Arabs pointed out that non-Jews, who later intermarried with Arabs, occupied the Biblical land of Canaan long before the Jews arrived. Arabs based their own claim on over thirteen centuries of occupation.

The early Jewish state of Judaea was overthrown by the Roman Emperor Titus in A.D. 70. For persistent rebellion against Rome, Jerusalem was burned to the ground in A.D. 135, and the city's Jews were either killed or deported. For almost two thousand years thereafter they were scattered throughout the world in what was called the Diaspora, each generation keeping alive the hope of an eventual return to the homeland of their ancestors. "Next year in Jerusalem," they toasted each other wistfully at Yom Kippur celebrations.

During twenty centuries of the Diaspora, Palestine fell under a succession of rulers — Romans, Greeks, Arabs, Crusaders, Saracens, Turks, and the British. But from the time of the Arab Empire until the twentieth century, the population of Palestine remained almost wholly Arabic.

In the Arab view, if Zionists could claim a "historical right" of the Jewish people to repossess the land where their ancestors had once lived, why couldn't the English demand a return of the United States to the British crown? Or the Italians, all the lands of the mighty Roman Empire?

The Zionist claim to Palestine was to some extent a claim of desperation. The Jewish people had suffered a chain of persecution at the hands of the Romans, the Crusaders, the Spanish Inquisition, and the Russian czars, all surpassed in cruelty and savagery by the German Nazis. The Zionists sought a homeland where Jews could be safe and free. For them it was a question of survival.

The Arabs had no quarrel with the Jewish right to a shelter from the anti-Semites of the world. In fact Feisal had declared, "We Arabs, especially the educated among us, look with the deepest sympathy on the Zionist movement." But the Arabs were angered by the Zionist attempt to take over an *Arab* land and dispossess the Arabs living there, creating a new Diaspora for the homeless Palestinians. Was one injustice to be rectified by creating another?

Ironically, one of the first people to suggest the Zionist idea was not a Jew but a Moslem. In 1873 the Shah of Persia, Nasir Al-Din, wrote in his diary during a visit to Europe, "The celebrated Rothschild, a Jew also, who is exceedingly rich, came to an audience, and we conversed with him. He greatly advocated the cause of the Jews. . . . I said to him: 'I have heard that you, brother, possess a thousand crores of money. I consider the best thing to do would be . . . pay fifty crores to some large or small State, and buy a territory in which you could collect all the Jews of the whole world, you becoming their chief, and leading them on their way in peace, so that you should no longer be thus scattered and dispersed.' We laughed heartily, and he made no reply."

Rothschild became one of the founders of Zionism.

The movement was given momentum in 1896 with the appearance of a book, *The Jewish State: An Attempt at a Modern Solution of the Jewish Question,* by a young Budapest-born Viennese lawyer, Theodore Herzl. "The Jewish State is essential to the world," he wrote; "it will therefore be created." To entice support from European governments, he declared: "For Europe we will create in Palestine an outpost against Asia; we will be the outpost of the civilized world against barbarity."

A year later Herzl called the First Zionist Congress in Basel, Switzerland, "to create for the Jewish people a home in Palestine secured by public law." Elected its first president, he was dismayed when many prominent Jews of the world rejected Zionism, on grounds that they had no interest in dividing their loyalties between their countries of residence and a projected Jewish nation in the Middle East.

Zionists at first imagined that the country they wished to settle was desolate and underpopulated. As early as 1881 pamphlets circulating in Romania described Palestine as virtually an empty wasteland. Jewish writer Israel Zangwill referred to it as "the land without people — for the people without land." Zionist leader Max Nordau was shocked when he discovered that this assumption was wrong.

"But there *are* Arabs in Palestine!" he exclaimed to Herzl. "I didn't know that! We're committing an injustice!"

To Herzl, however, the fellahin in the Palestinian countryside were either largely invisible or of no great consequence. Ironically, while visiting Egypt and becoming aware of widespread dissatisfaction among young Arab intellectuals, he noted in his diary, "These are the coming masters. It is a wonder that the English do not see this. They think they will be dealing with felahin forever."

Long-time Jewish residents of Palestine, a very different people from the Zionist immigrants of Europe, were not too sure they relished the idea of a Zionist homeland. Their ancestors were Sephardic Jews who had been expelled by the Spanish Inquisition in the late fifteenth and early sixteenth centuries. Welcomed in Palestine as a highly intelligent and educated people, they had been in great demand as secretaries, technicians, artisans, and dressmakers, and had risen to positions of influence in government circles. Their descendants now spoke Arabic, ate Arab food (except for non-kosher meat), enjoyed Arab music, wore their hair in long ringlets, and dressed as the Arabs did. Many had close Arab friends.

As the first Zionist immigrants began arriving in Palestine, conflicts arose over the land they settled. The first serious clash took place as early as 1886, when Arab farmers of the village of Yahudiya grew enraged by the newcomers' attempts to seal off purchased swampland, where fellahin cattle had grazed for centuries. The Arabs attacked the Jewish colonists, injuring five.

Struggle over the land marked the whole course of Zionist settlement, and as early as 1907 Jewish immigrants felt compelled to organize a home guard to protect their settlements against "Arab bandits." The Arabs, seeking to wrest their land from the Turks, felt threatened by each fresh wave of Jewish refugees escaping from European persecution.

"Two important phenomena of a similar nature, and yet opposed, at present manifest themselves in Asian Turkey," observed Naguib Azuri, a Jerusalem official, in 1905. "These are the awakening Arab nation and the latent efforts of the Jews to reconstitute on a very large scale the ancient kingdom of Israel. The two movements are destined to combat one another continuously until one is beaten by the other."

Upon the outcome of this struggle, he predicted, "will depend the fate of the entire world."

In 1911 the president of the Tenth Zionist Congress felt compelled to disavow any attempt to establish a Jewish nation in Palestine. The Zionists, he insisted, only wanted "not a Jewish state, but a home in the ancient land of our forefathers, where we can live a Jewish life without oppression."

David Ben-Gurion, the future father of Israel, was arrested in Jerusalem in 1915 as a Zionist agitator. Awaiting expulsion by the Turks, he met a young Arab friend he had studied law with at the University of Istanbul. When Ben-Gurion explained why he was under arrest, his friend said, "As your friend, I am deeply sorry. But as an Arab I am pleased."

"It came down on me like a blow," Ben-Gurion related afterward. "I said to myself, 'so there *is* an Arab national movement *here*. . . . It hit me like a bomb. I was completely dumfounded." Two years later, however, he still referred to Palestine as a country "in an historical and moral sense . . . without inhabitants."

After World War I, authority over Palestine was held by the British as a mandate. During the first year Sir Herbert Samuel, the high commissioner, put the Balfour Declaration into effect by allowing 16,500 Jews to enter the country. The Zionists were permitted to make major land purchases in seven Arab villages in Galilee, using funds donated by American and European Jews. Settlers protected their new region by organizing *Haganah* (Defense) as a strong guard force.

In 1921 Arab riots, burnings, and killings in half a dozen cities forced the British to reexamine the Balfour Declaration.

Samuel acceded to an Arab demand that the British suspend further Jewish immigration.

Worried, Weizmann told the London *Times*, "We do not seek to found a Zionist state. . . . We cannot hope to rule a country in which only one-seventh of the population at present are Jews. . . . By the establishment of the Jewish National Home we mean the creation of . . . Jewish institutions so that the country may become as quickly as possible as Jewish as England is English. . . . I see no reason for differences between us and the Arab non-Jewish population. There is plenty of room for us both in Palestine."

Weizmann's statement provoked new Arab protests, compelling the British government to challenge his interpretation of the Balfour Declaration. "Phrases have been used such as that Palestine is to become 'as Jewish as England is English,' " said Winston Churchill, secretary of state for the colonies. "His Majesty's Government regard any such expectation as impracticable and have no such aim in view. . . . The terms of the Declaration referred to do not contemplate that Palestine as a whole should be converted into a Jewish National Home, but that such a Home should be founded in Palestine."

Lord Edward Grey warned Parliament, "If ninety-three percent of the population of Palestine are Arabs, I do not see how you can establish other than an Arab Government without prejudice to their civil rights."

Seeking to defuse Arab anger in 1922, Churchill issued a White Paper that limited Jewish immigration into western Palestine; set aside Transjordan as an Arab kingdom under the Hashemites, with settlement there forbidden to Jews; and proclaimed Egypt independent, but with reservations that gave London the right to interfere in Egyptian affairs whenever this was considered necessary. In effect Egypt was kept as a British mandate under King Ahmed Fuad.

In the Arabian Peninsula, warfare broke out between Hussein and his arch-rival, Ibn Saud, leader of the Wahabi movement of religious zealotry. Saud detested the sherif of Mecca and his sons as impious, soft, decadent, and corrupt, and was determined to wrest the Holy Places from the grasp of the Hashemites. Saud's principal warrior was his son Faisal, an adept military commander and diplomat. Saud and Faisal were enraged in February 1924 when Hussein proclaimed himself caliph of all the Arab countries.

Attacking Mecca, they defeated the Hashemites and went on to conquer most of the Arabian Peninsula, uniting all tribal sheiks in a new nation called Saudi Arabia.

An important new Arab movement sprang up in Egypt in 1928, founded by an impassioned twenty-two-year-old teacher, Hassan al-Banna, who urged a back-to-the-Koran religious revival. Opposing all Western influences, he organized the fanatical Moslem Brotherhood, one of the most feared organizations in the Arab world.

Relations between Arabs and Jews worsened as the Jewish Agency, in charge of immigrant settlement, purchased more and more land in Palestine from absentee Syrian and Lebanese landlords. Arab farm workers, for whom there were few other jobs, were dispossessed. Riots broke out in 1929 when Zionists demonstrated at the Wailing Wall in Jerusalem, raising the Zionist flag and singing the Zionist anthem. In two weeks of violence 133 Jews and 116 Arabs were killed.

Investigating, the British Shaw Commission reported, "The Arabs have come to see in the Jewish immigrant not only a menace to their livelihood but a possible overlord of the future." The League of Nations decided that the Wailing Wall and the ground in front of it belonged to the Moslems, but that the Jews had the right of access to it for devotions, provided they did not use the wall as a backdrop for political rallies.

In 1930 stubborn Arab resistance by Syrians forced the French to yield to their demands for a Syrian republic. Two Syrian students in Paris, converted to socialism, organized the Baath — the Party of Renaissance. Michael Aflaq, a Christian, and Salah Bitar, a Moslem, asked Arab members to place their loyalties to a political party above the traditional Arab loyalties to family, tribe, and religion. Baath branches sprang up in Syria, Iraq, and Lebanon.

With the rise to power of the Nazis in Germany in 1932, new millions of Jews sought to flee persecution. Responding to the emergency, the Zionists stepped up their efforts to develop Palestine as a Jewish national home. New farm settlements of immigrants sprang up with incredible speed.

At daybreak, members of a kibbutz would move into purchased land and erect a defense tower by sunrise. A colony wall would be up by noon. Before the sun set the colonists would have organized a farm commune, complete with chickens and cows. The Arabs, astonished and dismayed as these settlements suddenly appeared in their midst, fought the colonists.

In 1935 militants in the Haganah organized their own guerrilla force of five thousand men. Called the Irgun Zvai, it began making reprisal raids on Arab communities. Weizmann deplored "the tragic, futile, un-Jewish resort to terrorism, a perversion of the purely defensive function of Haganah."

The Mufti of Jerusalem called a general Arab strike to compel the British to halt Jewish immigration. Seeking conciliation, Ben-Gurion met with Arab nationalist leaders to propose creating a self-governing Jewish territory within a federation of independent Arab states. He promised large-scale Zionist aid to help the Arabs develop Palestine.

"I prefer the country to remain desolate for another hundred years," replied Musa Alami coolly, "until we Arabs are capable of developing it ourselves." Ben-Gurion admitted later, "If I were an Arab I would say the same." He told the Arabs, "For us it is a question of existence, of life and death. We have come here and shall come here whether there will or will not be Arab-Jewish understanding. Riots will not stop us."

Ignoring the Arab general strike, the British government in Palestine increased the Jewish immigration quota to allow in more German refugees. Infuriated, the Arabs intensified their resistance to the level of civil war.

"The Arabs have been driven into a state verging on despair," an Arab spokesman declared, "and the present unrest is no more than an expression of that despair."

Rushing in troop reinforcements, the British arrested Arab leaders and issued arms to the Jewish community.

By this time Nazi propaganda had begun to penetrate the Middle East, inflaming Arab grievances against both the Jews and England. In Egypt a fascist group called the Green Shirts collaborated with the Moslem Brotherhood in demanding total freedom from British control.

When King Fuad of Egypt died in 1936, his sixteen-year-old son Farouk was brought home from school in England to rule through a regency council. Hopeful that a better day was dawning for them, Egyptians welcomed him with demonstrations of joy.

"To us he was a young god," recalled Hafiz Khittab, a worker on Fuad's estates. "Have you ever seen thousands of beggars cheering, and the fellahin giving up a day's work in their fields for a king? They did on that day, forgetting their misery and their hunger and the poverty in the villages. We even forgave Fuad, the hated, the tight-fisted and cruel, for such a son. . . . The English? He would take them and all other infidels off our backs. . . . That day — his day — we felt was the first day of our freedom."

Britain appeased Egyptian unrest by signing a new Anglo-

Egyptian treaty giving Egypt nominal independence, abolishing extraterritorial rights for foreigners, and letting Egypt represent itself in the League of Nations. The fine print of the treaty, however, let Britain keep armed forces in the Suez Canal zone, and occupy the country in case of war.

The British also agreed to help build an all-Egyptian army. Previously only sons of the Turkish elite had been permitted to attend the Egyptian Royal Military Academy. Now it was opened to Arab youths of every class. Among the new cadets admitted in 1936 were two youths from plebian backgrounds, Gamal Abdel Nasser and Anwar Sadat, who were one day to join in driving the British out of Egypt.

In 1937 the British sent the Peel Commission to investigate the trouble in Palestine. It reported, "About 1,000,000 Arabs are in strife, open or latent, with some 400,000 Jews. There is no common ground between them. The Arab community is predominantly Asiatic in character, the Jewish community predominantly European. . . . The War [World War I] and its sequel have inspirited all Arabs with the hope of reviving in a free and united Arab world the traditions of the Arab golden age. The Jews [are] similarly inspired by their historic past."

The report concluded gloomily, "The conflict will go on, the gulf between Arabs and Jews will widen." The Peel Commission recommended partitioning Palestine between them.

Arab leaders rejected the proposal, and in a new wave of Arab terrorism, British officials were murdered. The British rounded up and deported Arab leaders, dynamited houses of suspected terrorists, swept almost a thousand Arabs into concentration camps, and hanged some found with forbidden firearms. The Mufti escaped to Lebanon, where the French permitted him to continue directing the Arab revolt.

By the summer of 1938 guerrilla warfare had all but paralyzed government in Palestine. Arab paramilitary forces had invaded and captured important towns. To fight off their raids, the British trained members of Haganah as "Special Night Squads." Irgun terrorists among them defied Haganah control, launching their own attacks on Arab communities.

In 1939 the British government issued a White Paper decreeing that after ten years Palestine was to become an independent, bi-national state, with Arabs and Jews sharing in the government. Meanwhile, as a concession to the Arab revolt, severe limitations were placed on Jewish immigration and land transfers to Jews. The Zionists were outraged at what they considered a flagrant betrayal of the Balfour Declaration.

Haganah, stung by criticism that its policy of restraint had failed, now began to cooperate with the Irgun, which was making terrorist attacks on British government buildings. Haganah initiated illegal anti-British broadcasts over the Voice of Israel, and smuggled in boatloads of forbidden immigrants under the noses of British port authorities.

But with the outbreak of World War II, the Zionists had second thoughts. How could they continue opposing the British, who were now fighting the Jews' worst enemy, Nazi Germany?

# 8

# Israel Is Born

STOPPING ITS ILLEGAL BROADCASTS, Haganah agreed to help the British war effort. Irgun followed suit when the British agreed to free Irgun political prisoners. But one Irgun commander, Abraham Stern, remained adamantly anti-British, refusing to cooperate. He broke away a band of three hundred Jewish terrorists who continued their harassment as the Stern gang.

In April 1940 the Mufti entered a secret agreement with Germany to raise Arab armies against the British in the Middle East. Toward this end he hatched a plot in conspiracy with the Moslem Brotherhood and the Free Officers of Egypt, a secret revolutionary society within the Egyptian army.

The plot misfired. Anwar Sadat, who with Nasser was one of the Free Officers' leaders, said later, "If ill-luck had not so dogged our enterprise, we might have struck a quick blow at the

British, joining forces with the Axis, and changed the course of events.''

The British Eighth Army made Egypt its headquarters for the desert fight against Nazi General Erwin Rommel. The renewed occupation of Egypt intensified Arab hatred of the British, who treated Egyptians with scorn as "Wogs" and "Gypos." They openly mocked King Farouk, who by now had become a great embarrassment to his people.

Irascible, violent, unpredictable, the king was obsessed with personal pleasures. Gluttony had made him enormously fat, which did not prevent him from pursuing women at wild parties. Flinging money away gambling, he once lost $250,000 in a single night. He explained his appointment of an unqualified minister of justice: "I like his mustache." Warned about the will of the people, he sneered, "The will of the people emanates from *my* will!"

The Free Officers secretly vowed that Farouk must be dumped from the throne of Egypt as soon as possible.

When the Axis forces had been driven from Africa, the British permitted the Egyptian premier, Nahas Pasha, to call a conference of Arab leaders in Alexandria in July 1943. They agreed to form a new Arab League, uniting behind a demand for total postwar independence.

Ibn Saud called upon President Franklin D. Roosevelt to promise that no action would be taken by the Allies on Palestine without consulting the Arab League first. Agreeing, Roosevelt asked the king what he thought ought to be done to help the Jewish victims of Nazi Germany.

"Give them and their descendants the choicest lands and homes," Ibn Saud replied, "of the Germans who oppressed them."

When it became clear that the Axis powers would lose the war, the Arab states abandoned their neutrality and declared war on Germany. By becoming allies of the Western powers, they strengthened their claim to Arab independence and an Arab Palestine. The Mufti lost his influence as an Arab leader by fleeing to Berlin and broadcasting propaganda for the Nazis.

As the war drew to a close, Zionist extremists sought to defy the British White Paper of 1939 and open Palestine completely to Jewish immigration. In January 1944 the Irgun called for revolt, declaring, "There is no longer any armistice between the Jewish people and the British Administration in Eretz Israel which hands our brothers over to Hitler. . . . This, then, is our demand: Immediate transfer of power in Eretz Israel to a Provisional Hebrew Government."

The Irgun's battle cry was echoed by the Stern gang: "We shall fight, every Jew in the Homeland will fight. The God of Israel, the Lord of Hosts, will aid us." But the Jewish Agency and its military arm, Haganah, repudiated this call for open battle against the British. The moderate Zionists hoped that the United States would be able to compel Britain to reopen Palestine to Jewish immigration.

In August Jewish terrorists attempted to assassinate the British high commissioner, and raided arms dumps, banks, and communications facilities. In November the British minister of state, Lord Moyne, was murdered in Cairo by two members of the Stern gang.

The Arab League was legally established in March 1945, its first six members those countries that had become independent since 1919 — Egypt, Syria, Iraq, Transjordan, Saudi Arabia, and Yemen. Egyptian leadership was acknowledged with the establishment of a permanent secretariat in Cairo.

The League set three goals for itself — to rekindle Arab pride by reviving the ancient glories of Arabism throughout the Middle East; to offset the Zionist lobby by making the Arab cause understood in the West; and to compel Western respect for the Arab nations as a united bloc. The Egyptian government set an example by wringing a promise from the British to withdraw their troops from Egypt by March 1947.

As though awakening from a sleep of centuries, the Arabs now felt that they no longer had to submit to domination or control by Europe, which emerged from the war weak and exhausted. Newly independent Arab states had equality in the UN with the world's richest and most powerful countries.

Postwar revelations that the Nazis had put to death six million Jews appalled the Arabs, despite their conflict with Zionism. Nazi prisoners of war in Egypt were labeled swine by Arab officers, and on prisoner records were forced to describe their occupation simply as "murderer."

President Harry S. Truman, despite Roosevelt's pledge to Ibn Saud, publicly urged the British government to admit one hundred thousand Jewish refugees to Palestine at once. Tensions soared in the Middle East. Jewish terrorists struck at British and Arab targets in the cities. Arab terrorists fought from the hills against the British and Jews. Both Arabs and Jews reserved their hardest blows for the British, seeking to drive them out of Palestine, then fight each other for control.

The weary British appealed to the UN to relieve them of the responsibility for Palestine. In November 1947 the UN decided that the British mandate should end within eight months, after which Palestine should be divided into independent Jewish and Arab states linked together in an economic union.

The Zionists, who now owned about six percent of the land and constituted a third of the population, were awarded fifty-six percent of the country. The Arabs, with forty-six percent of the land and sixty-six percent of the population, were allotted forty-three percent of Palestine for their state. Both the United States and the Soviet Union supported the UN plan; Britain abstained from voting. The Jewish Agency accepted the compromise. The Arab League attacked it bitterly as unjust.

Fresh fighting broke out in Palestine. An exodus of Arabs began from areas allocated to the future state of Israel. The Zionists claimed that the émigrés were ordered to leave temporarily by their absent leaders in broadcasts from Damascus, in order to give Arab armies free reign to attack, and also to prove to the world that Palestinians would not live under Israeli rule. The Arabs charged that the refugees had been expelled by the Zionists or frightened off by terrorism.

During the first three months of 1948, according to the Palestinians, Zionist terrorists indiscriminately killed or maimed over eleven hundred Arab men, women, and children in marketplaces, cafés, hotels, apartment houses, villages, and on buses and trains. When Palestinians fled, Haganah forces occupied their properties, then turned them over to Jewish squatters.

"The panic of one village infected the next," observed *New York Times* correspondent Dana Adams Schmidt, "until whole groups of villages were evacuated." An Irgun spokesman justified his organization's resort to terror tactics: "It is the only way. We have no other weapon that will move the British and frighten the Arabs. But believe me, it is not out of hatred for them — only out of love for our own people."

Palestinian leaders appealed to other Arab leaders to back their cause with arms as fervently as the Zionists supported the Israelis. But most Arabs had little desire to fight, wanting merely to be left to till their fields and tend their olive trees in peace. The Arab League, split by rivalries, did little more than pass resolutions condemning partition.

When Palestinian leader Musa Alami toured the Middle East seeking Arab support, the prime minister of Iraq assured him that all he needed to drive the Zionists out was "a few brooms."

The president of Syria confided that there was nothing to worry about because Syria had an atomic bomb "made locally; we fortunately found a very clever fellow, a tinsmith."

King Abdullah of Transjordan was determined to swallow as much of Palestine as he could for himself, with as little fighting as possible. The principal aim of Egyptian leaders was to stop Abdullah. Musa Alami gloomily reached the conclusion that Palestine would become the state of Israel because the Arab world had no united will to resist, no unified administration, no leadership. Arab states that had already won their independence were guarding it jealously, unwilling to set nationalism aside for the sake of a united Arab power.

The fanatical Mufti, now in Cairo, stepped into the breach with a call for Holy War, crying, "No compromise with the Jews!" His Arab Higher Committee organized a series of bombings and attacks on Jewish convoys in and around Jerusalem, Tel Aviv, and Haifa. The Haganah replied in kind.

The Arab League finally organized an Arab liberation army made up largely of the Moslem Brotherhood. Striking from Egypt, these guerrilla forces made hit-and-run raids against the Jewish agricultural communes known as kibbutzim.

The Irgun and Stern gangs struck back fiercely. In one particularly violent raid on April 9, 1948, their combined force captured the Arab village of Deir Yassin. Some two hundred fifty unarmed civilians, including many women and children, were killed. Their bodies were thrown into the village well and captives were paraded in chains through the Jewish quarter of Jerusalem. Twenty of these hostages were executed in a stone quarry.

The massacre at Deir Yassin intensified the Arab flight from Palestine, bringing to over three hundred thousand the number who had left their homes in the area designated for the future state of Israel. The Arabs bitterly accused Haganah of staging the massacre to panic the Arab population into a wholesale exodus.

Denying it had authorized the raid, Haganah pointed out that the Arabs had murdered just as many Jewish civilians. The fault, said Haganah, was the Arabs' for rejecting all attempts at settlement. Arab leaders replied wrathfully that one did not negotiate with terrorists who had no business in Palestine in the first place.

The fighting raged to new heights as the British began withdrawing their troops. On May 14, 1948, David Ben-Gurion officially ended the British mandate by proclaiming the establishment of the state of Israel. The British White Paper restricting Jewish immigration and purchase of land was annulled. One day later the British officially withdrew their forces from the new nation.

At 5:25 A.M. an Egyptian plane bombed Tel Aviv. Simultaneously an Egyptian army invaded Palestine from the south, the Arab Legion from Transjordan in the east, and Syrian and Lebanese forces from the north. Thirteen hours after Israel had been proclaimed a nation, an Arab world torn by rivalry had suddenly united in haste to topple it.

"Our security made it necessary for us to defend the frontiers of our Arab Brethren with whom we were destined to live in one and the same region," later explained Nasser, then an officer in the Egyptian army. Arafat, who also fought in the 1948 War, said, "It was a fight to defend our existence."

Better-organized, well-trained Haganah forces outfought the Arabs on all fronts. Egyptian generalship was poor, leaving the Arab armies uncoordinated, badly armed and supplied. After a month of fierce fighting, the UN dispatched Count Folke Bernadotte of the Swedish Red Cross to mediate a cease-fire.

Arranging a truce on June 11, he reported to the UN, "The right of innocent people, uprooted from their homes by the present terror and ravages of war, to be returned to their homes should be affirmed. . . . The liability of the provisional government of Israel to restore private property to its private owners and to indemnify those owners for property wantonly destroyed is clear."

Fighting broke out again on July 8. But the Arab armies were now so hopelessly disorganized that in ten more days of war the Israeli forces swept across the country, occupying fifty percent more land than the UN had allotted to them. Almost a million Palestinians were now in full flight.

The Israelis had won total victory.

On July 15 Bernadotte arranged a second stand-in-place truce which saved fifteen thousand Egyptian troops, including Nasser, who were trapped between Israeli forces. Defying the UN, King Farouk refused to accept the truce.

The Stern gang was outraged at Bernadotte for recommending that Israel must permit Arab refugees to return home and collect compensation for property damage. On September 20, members of the gang murdered Bernadotte in the streets of Jerusalem. He was succeeded as head of the UN Palestine Mission by his American aide, Ralph Bunche.

Shock waves of defeat rocked the Arab world. Arabs everywhere were disillusioned by the contrast between boastful prewar threats of Arab leaders, and their woeful weakness on the field of battle. Musa Alami, who had helped to found the Arab League, said bitterly, "In the face of the enemy, the Arabs were . . . each fearing and anxiously watching the other and intriguing against it. What concerned them most and guided their policy was not to win the war and save Palestine from the enemy, but . . . who would be predominant in Palestine, or annex it to themselves." Nasser brooded over "how we were cheated into a war unprepared, and how our destinies have been the plaything of passions, plots and greed."

Arab leaders were equally embittered at the West, which they accused of using Israel as a pawn to establish a non-Arab imperialist stronghold in the Middle East. Arab feelings of inferiority, instilled by centuries of subjugation by the Turks, British, and French, were freshly aroused by the humiliation of being beaten in the 1948 War.

The new state of Israel governed 167,000 Arabs who still remained in their territory with the same regulations the British had used to keep Zionist terrorists under control. Arabs needed passes to travel, and were not allowed to visit certain areas or to market their produce.

The great mass of refugees fled to Syria, Transjordan, and the Egyptian-occupied Gaza Strip. Almost a million people had been made homeless and penniless wanderers, living on day-to-day charity. Tents provided by the Red Cross and voluntary charities were far too few, forcing as many as a dozen people to huddle under a single tent to keep dry in rainy weather.

When King Abdullah occupied the Palestinian West Bank of the River Jordan, his enlarged nation shortened its name to Jordan. With its huge new refugee population, the Hashemite desert kingdom became a semi-Palestinian state, refugees actually outnumbering native Bedouin. Jordan was the only Arab state that granted the refugees full citizenship.

Responsibility for the six hundred thousand who were lodged in West Bank camps, however, was assumed by the UN Relief and Works Agency (UNRWA), which also took over supervision of refugee camps in the Gaza Strip, Syria, and Lebanon. If the establishment of Israel meant the end of the Jewish Diaspora, for the Arabs of Palestine it meant the beginning of a Moslem one.

Jewish immigrants were now arriving in Israel in numbers equal to the Arabs displaced. Declaring the land and homes of those Arabs "abandoned," the Israeli government turned them over to the Jewish newcomers. An estimated forty percent of Arab holdings were confiscated in this manner.

Zionists defended Israel's refusal to allow Arabs to return to their homes on grounds of national security. To repatriate them, Zionists argued, would incorporate within Israel a fifth column of vengeful Arabs intent upon destroying the new state. The Arabs charged that the real reasons were to hold on to confiscated property, and to keep a Jewish majority in the voting population.

Despite the UN truce, sporadic fighting continued through late 1948. The Israelis attacked Arab border villages, accusing them of harboring Fedayeen terrorists. Many Arabs who were forcibly expelled from their homes filed complaints with Amnesty International, a highly respected and impartial agency. Investigations verified their charges as true.

The British, worried about damage to the Suez Canal, threatened Israel to intervene on Egypt's side if the fighting did not stop. Egypt and Israel then quickly agreed to respect the UN truce. The Egyptians wanted no more British occupation disguised as "protection." Speaking for Israel, Ben-Gurion said, "Well, we can take on six Arab countries but we really can't take on the British Empire, too."

The war finally ended. But the struggle between the Arab nations and their new neighbor was only beginning.

# 9

# Nasser Challenges the West

IN THE FINAL ARMISTICE between Israel and the Arab states signed in July 1949, Egypt was given the Gaza Strip while Jordan annexed the West Bank of Palestine, including the old city of Jerusalem, all crowded with refugees.

Fearful that Israel secretly planned even further expansion to include all Arab land that once had been Jewish in Biblical times, the Arab League imposed an economic boycott on Israel in hopes of starving the new nation out. The boycott failed because Western nations, particularly the United States, ignored it, continuing to supply the Israelis.

In 1950 the Israelis sought to give a legal patina to their confiscation of Arab property by passing an "emergency decree on the property of absentees." Troubled, Rabbi R. Benjamin wrote, "We will sooner or later have to tell the truth: we have no moral right to prevent the Arab refugees from returning to their homeland. . . . We have no right to occupy the house of an Arab unless we pay an adequate price for it. The same goes for his fields, orchards, shops and workshops. We have no right to create a national enclave and pursue Zionist ideals at the expense of other people's property. To do so amounts to committing robbery.''

Israeli kibbutzim used another technique for annexing Arab land. Settlers on the border drove tractors in ever widening sweeps at their field boundaries, extending their cultivation into Arab farmland. Armored vehicles of the Israeli border police prevented Arab villagers from driving them off.

On July 20, 1951, King Abdullah of Jordan paid with his life for having agreed to a truce with the Israelis, in exchange for his annexation of the West Bank. He was assassinated in Jerusalem by a Palestinian terrorist in the horrified presence of his young son Hussein, who succeeded him.

Another king marked for elimination was Farouk of Egypt. Captain Gamal Abdel Nasser, who headed the central committee of the secret Society of Free Officers, circulated leaflets urging Farouk's overthrow. He led an unsuccessful attempt to assassinate the army's commanding general.

The Free Officers staged their coup against Farouk on July 23, 1952. Seizing Cairo, they arrested Farouk, his ministers and generals. The king was sent into exile.

"People of Egypt," Anwar Sadat said over Radio Cairo, "Egypt has lived through one of the darkest periods of its history. The army has been tainted by the agents of dissolution. This was one of the causes of our defeat in Palestine. Led by fools, traitors and incompetents, the army was incapable of defending Egypt. This is why we have carried out a purge. The army is now in the hands of men in whose ability, integrity and patriotism you can have complete confidence."

At first Nasser was content to remain in the background of the bloodless coup. General Mohammed Naguib, a respected and popular war hero, was allowed to head the new military government. Naguib forestalled any possible British intervention by assuring London that British lives and property would be fully protected.

In October 1954 Nasser scored a diplomatic triumph as the power behind the scenes, getting Britain to sign a new Anglo-Egyptian treaty under which the British pledged to withdraw all their troops from the Suez zone within twenty months. Next day a banner with Nasser's signature, raised over Cairo, told Egyptians: "Lift up your head, comrade. The days of oppression are over!"

The Moslem Brotherhood, however, attacked him as a traitor because the treaty contained a clause reserving Britain's right to reoccupy Egypt if war threatened the canal. On October 24 a Brotherhood fanatic attempted to assassinate Nasser at a public meeting in Alexandria. Nasser outlawed the organization and confiscated its arms. Six members were hanged in Cairo's prison. Thousands were arrested, hundreds tortured.

General Naguib, who was alleged to have been implicated in the conspiracy, was placed under arrest. Nasser was now in full and undisputed control of the government.

An ambitious leader, he hoped to make Cairo the capital of an Islamic world community of over four hundred million Moslems. In April 1955 he sought to propagate this concept at the Bandung Conference of neutral Third World nations in Indonesia, without success. But he was impressed by the Third World policy of staying nonaligned in the Cold War between the United States and the Soviet Union, winning economic assistance by shrewdly playing off one side against another.

This became Nasser's policy for Egypt. No longer, he de-

cided, would the dark-skinned races of the world allow themselves to be used as pawns in white men's power struggles. Now
the darker races would manipulate Westerners to build better
lives for themselves, instead of dying for causes not their own.
Playing off Moscow against Washington, he obtained loans for
agricultural and irrigation projects badly needed to increase food
for Egypt's rapidly swelling masses.

To curb the population explosion, he opened birth control
centers all over the country. "The Egyptian revolution will not
enable us to raise our standard of living and that of our children," warned the government daily *Al Goumhouriya* in December 1955, "as long as the threat of an ever-increasing population remains hanging over our heads."

Nasser began reshaping the social and economic structure of
Egypt. Purging corrupt politicians, he also broke the power of
the rich landowning oligarchy with new laws that restricted all
land holdings to a maximum of two hundred acres. Over half a
million acres of confiscated lands were divided up among poor
fellahin, for whom whole new villages were built. New apartment houses were built for the urban poor.

All titles were abolished, leveling distinction between rich
beys and poor fellahin. While emphasizing that his brand of
socialism was Arab in nature, not Marxist, Nasser nationalized
Egypt's banks, insurance companies, and industries.

Appalled conservatives called him a Communist; suspicious
Communists assailed him as a dictator. But although the media
were censored, educated Egyptians had little difficulty in learning what was going on at home and abroad. And although Nasser's secret police kept an eye on all political opposition, public
criticism was tolerated.

Seeking to unite the Arab world behind him, Nasser was torn
between two strategies. The first he called "unity of

purpose" — uniting Syria, Iraq, and Algeria, the left-wing Arab countries, to work for social revolution, in opposition to such conservative Arab states as Saudi Arabia and Jordan.

The second strategy he called "unity of ranks" — uniting with *all* Arab nations against the Western powers. His policies wavered back and forth between the two strategies.

Exploiting Cold War rivalry, he won an offer from Moscow to supply Egypt with new weapons to modernize the Egyptian army, in exchange for payment in cotton and rice. The Russians also agreed to help industrialize Egypt, and to build a huge dam at Aswan to provide irrigation for desert farms as well as hydroelectric power for new industries.

With Moscow's offer for the dam under his belt, Nasser invited Washington to better it. Secretary of State John Foster Dulles declined "in view of Egypt's unstable economy." Indignant, Nasser jolted the United States by announcing the deal to buy sophisticated arms from the Communist world.

In January 1956 Nasser legalized his power by introducing a constitution that made Egypt a republic, with a president elected for a six-year term by a national assembly. In June he was unanimously elected the republic's first president.

The Soviet Union sent over fifteen hundred technicians and advisors to Cairo, the first bastion of Russian influence in the Middle East. But when the Russians realized that the Aswan High Dam would take ten years to build and cost 1.3 billion dollars, they began to back away from that part of the bargain.

Disappointed, Nasser once more approached the United States, asking for a two-hundred-million-dollar loan to begin the dam. Dulles, now worried by the Soviet presence in Cairo, as Nasser knew he would be, this time agreed. A jubilant Nasser stirred the Egyptian people with enthusiastic predictions about the great changes the Aswan High Dam would make in their lives.

He was stunned when Dulles, for political reasons, suddenly changed his mind, expressing public doubt that the Egyptian economy was capable of carrying through the project successfully. Caught out on a limb after the grandiose promises he had made to the Egyptian people about the dam, Nasser was further humiliated by Dulles's tactless public insult. The American secretary of state had caused him to lose face before his own people, before all Arabs, before the whole world.

In fury he struck out at the only major Western target available to him — the Suez Canal. On July 26, 1956, he announced that he was nationalizing the Anglo-French Suez Canal Company, and would use its thirty-million-dollar annual profit to build a fund to pay for the Aswan Dam. He accused Dulles of refusing the loan because Egypt would not submit to Israeli domination and forsake the Palestinian refugees.

"Americans, choke on your fury!" he cried out publicly. "For you will not be able to dominate us or control our existence! . . . We have pride in Arabism, and our land cannot be sold for money!" He told a *Look* magazine reporter privately, "When you said you would not build the High Dam, we had to show you that you cannot insult a small country and get away with it. If we had accepted the slap in the face, you would have slapped us again."

The loss of the canal was a crippling blow to Britain and France. Neither could survive long economically without the Middle East oil and Asian trade which flowed through it. Neither country relished being at Nasser's mercy, and France was already incensed at him for providing aid to anti-French rebels in Algeria. In England, when aides suggested a plan to "neutralize" Nasser, Prime Minister Anthony Eden shouted, "I want him *destroyed,* can't you understand? I want him removed!"

Israel, too, was anxious to see an end of the Egyptian firebrand who permitted suicide squads of Fedayeen to raid Israeli settlements from the Gaza Strip; who prevented ships with cargoes to and from Israel from using the Gulf of Aqaba; and whose Soviet arms threatened Israeli survival.

In secret consultation, England, France, and Israel plotted Nasser's overthrow. On October 29, 1956, the Israelis invaded Egyptian territory, bombing airfields and landing troops at Port Said and in the canal zone. Next day, according to plan, Britain and France ordered "both" Egypt and Israel to withdraw ten miles on each side of the canal. For the Egyptians that meant retreating and abandoning all of the Sinai, leaving the Israelis more than a hundred miles inside Egyptian territory.

The ultimatum provoked furious riots all over the Arab world. The UN Security Council met hastily, passing a resolution that called upon Israel to withdraw from the Sinai, and on all member nations to refrain from using force. It was vetoed by England and France, who next day began to bomb Egypt. On November 5 they invaded the canal zone with paratroops and commandos. Before they could capture the canal, however, Nasser sank ships in the locks to block it.

The Israelis seized almost all of the Sinai peninsula, including the Gaza Strip, where they wiped out Fedayeen bases that had been harassing the kibutzim. The Palestinians bitterly accused Israeli forces of arbitrarily massacring civilians in the refugee camps along with commandos.

The fighting in the Sinai ended with over a thousand Egyptian soldiers killed and six thousand taken prisoner, at a loss of only 181 dead and one prisoner for the Israelis.

World opinion was shocked by so flagrant an act of old-style imperialism. Led by the United States, the UN demanded immediate withdrawal of the invaders. The Soviet Union even hinted darkly that if England and France refused, Russian guided missiles might fall on their population centers.

The British and French reluctantly withdrew their forces. The Israelis, however, held on stubbornly to the Gaza Strip.

Historian Arnold Toynbee visited the Gaza Strip while it was in their hands. "There are plenty of fanatics and plenty of prisoners in the Gaza Strip today," he wrote. "Their tempers are on edge, and I would not put it beyond them to attempt some desperate act of demolition that might bring, not just a single temple or theatre, but the whole of civilization tumbling in ruin about the ears of the human race. . . . The refugees have nothing to do but to brood over the injustice that has been done to them. The Germans wronged the Jews, but the Arabs, not the Germans, have been made to pay."

Ben-Gurion finally agreed to withdraw the Israeli army after Egypt acknowledged Israel's right of passage through the Gulf of Aqaba, and consented to the stationing of a UN Expeditionary Force (UNEF) between Gaza and Israel to prevent any further raids by the Fedayeen.

When the Egyptians were once more in possession of the Gaza Strip, however, Radio Cairo threatened, "The Gulf of Aqaba will [continue to be] closed to Israeli ships, and our Fedayeen will continue to sow terror in Israel."

Far from destroying Nasser, as the Anglo-French-Israeli plot had intended, the brief Suez War made him both a martyr and a hero in the eyes of the Arab world. All over the Middle East café owners displayed photos of the Arab leader who had wrested the Suez Canal away from the British and French imperialists, and who had compelled world opinion to force them and the Israelis out of Egypt.

Nasser's new prestige now made him the unquestioned leader of the Arab world. New hopes rose for pan-Arabic unity. Nasser began referring to himself as an Arab, something educated Egyptians seldom did because they felt superior to desert tribesmen and semi-Orientals. Other Arab leaders, compelled to acknowledge Egypt's primacy, were at the same time wary of Nasser's personal ambitions and radicalism.

Pro-Nasser movements in conservative Arab countries worked for revolution. In 1957 an attempted coup in Jordan, supported by Palestinian refugees, failed to overthrow Hussein. The king blamed Nasser's intrigues. King Saud was reported to have offered ten million dollars to Colonel Abdul Hamid Sarraj, head of Syrian Intelligence, to arrange Nasser's murder.

UNRWA sought to get the Palestinian refugees out of their miserable camps by resettling them permanently in other Arab lands. The Arab governments balked, claiming this would signify surrender of the Palestinians' right to return to their own homes. UNRWA authorities then did their best to provide good educational opportunities for children in the camps.

"To what purpose?" demanded Palestinian headmen bitterly. "What have these children to look forward to when they are educated?" Refugee youths grew up indoctrinated by their elders with one burning resolve — to regain their homeland, no matter how many generations of Palestinians it took.

In the summer of 1957 a dozen Palestinian leaders from Syria, Gaza, Iraq, Jordan, and Lebanon met in Kuwait to form Al Fatah ("Conquest"), a Fedayeen organization dedicated to liberating Palestine at all costs and by all methods.

"We wait and wait and wait for the justice of the United States, for the justice of the world," Al Fatah chief Yasir Arafat told Dana Adams Schmidt, "while our people are suffering in the tents and caves. But nothing of this was realized. Our dispersion was aggravated. . . . The only way to return to our homes and our land is the armed struggle."

Their strategy called for compelling world attention by daring and shocking acts that would make international headlines, while at the same time dragging the Arab nations into renewed hostilities against the Israelis.

Hostilities were already flaring in the demilitarized zone between Israel and Syria. The trouble, according to Major General Carl von Horn, Swedish chief of staff to the UN Truce Supervisory Organization, resulted from the Israeli determination to occupy all demilitarized zones around their borders, "and to get all Arabs out of the way by fair means or foul." The Israelis were found guilty of violating the armistice agreement at a meeting of the UN Mixed Armistice Commission (MAC), which they refused to attend.

Syria was also having problems with the Russians, who, having given the country arms and two hundred million dollars in loans, were making it clear that they now expected Syria to behave as a Soviet satellite. The alarmed leaders of the Baath party, Aflaq and Bitar, led a delegation to Cairo to urge Nasser to thwart the Russians by joining Syria to Egypt in a United Arab Republic (UAR). Nasser quickly agreed when they submitted to his leadership, with the UAR's capital in Cairo.

The union was formalized on January 14, 1958, as overjoyed Arab crowds chanted a new song: "I am Egyptian and you are Syrian. I am Syrian and you are Egyptian." Appealing to other Arab states to join the UAR, Nasser declared, "The victory of Arab nationalism means the end of foreign influence and the beginning of . . . a great state in this part of the world which will bring back the first glorious days of Saladin, days in which Arab nationalism united Arabs everywhere."

Pro-Nasser rebels in Lebanon mounted a revolt against pro-American President Camille Chamoun, who accused Syria of supplying them with funds and arms on Nasser's orders. Chamoun pleaded for American help under the Eisenhower Doctrine, which Dulles had formulated to aid any Middle East country that felt itself threatened by "international Communism."

American marines landed on the beaches of Lebanon in July. UN Secretary-General Dag Hammarskjold angrily demanded an explanation from the UN's American ambassador. Seeking to justify the intervention, Henry Cabot Lodge asked Dulles for proof that the UAR was interfering in Lebanon's internal affairs.

"I was surprised to learn," Lodge wrote later, "that such information was not available." In a UN debate the United States was denounced for interfering in a Middle East civil war to prop up a government favorable to American interests.

But Washington could take some comfort in a growing rift between Nasser and the Communist world. In November the Syrian and Iraqi Communist parties began attacking Egyptian rule in Syria as "undemocratic." Replying with a slashing attack on the Communists as enemies of Arab nationalism and unity, Nasser ordered mass arrests of his opponents in the UAR.

Furious at the Soviet Union for permitting an open Communist challenge to his authority, Nasser sought to mend his relations with the United States. At the same time, however, he refused to lift the blockade of Israeli cargoes through the Suez Canal. The United States Senate deliberated taking action against the blockade, but Senator William Fulbright, chairman of the Foreign Relations Committee, advised against it.

"What it will accomplish," he told the Senate, "is to annoy the Arabs and fortify them in their conviction that in any issue arising from the Arab-Israeli controversy, the United States, because of domestic political pressures, will be on the side of the Israelis. This Arab conviction, for which I regret to say history affords some justification, is the greatest single burden which American diplomacy has to carry in the Middle East."

In September 1960 Nasser came to the UN to plead the case of the Palestinians. Meeting Eisenhower, he declared that the UAR wanted friendship with the United States, but that the

American supply of arms to Israel was an obstacle. Eisenhower found the Egyptian leader "impressive, tall, straight, strong, positive." Nasser felt confident that his visit had warmed up Arab relations with the West considerably.

His relations with his junior partners, the Syrians, grew steadily chillier, however. Fed up with Egyptian arrogance, in September 1961 a junta of Syrian army officers revolted against the UAR. Reestablishing Syrian independence, they ordered all Egyptians to leave the country. Nasser was forced to withdraw them, explaining, "Arabs cannot fight Arabs."

However, by the following spring he had concluded that his Egyptian brand of socialism and his dream of a revived Arab Empire were being denied to the Arab people by their selfish, shortsighted leaders. He determined to get rid of those leaders.

"The concept of Arab unity," he declared, "no longer requires meetings of the Arab Nation to portray solidarity among governments." That solidarity would come from the people themselves. Egyptians must issue the call, he said, "without hesitating for one moment before the outworn argument that this would be considered interference in the affairs of others."

He began actively subverting other Arab governments, infiltrating them with a network of Egyptian agents to foment revolt. Counting on his popularity with the Arab masses and reformist army officers, he appealed for their support over the heads of their governments.

Syria angrily called a meeting of the Arab League in August 1962 to consider charges that Nasser was interfering in Syrian internal affairs. The meeting grew so stormy that police had to be called in. Nasser threatened to pull out of the League if Syria was not censured, rather than Egypt. The League called off the meeting to avoid an open Arab split.

Nasser-inspired revolution broke out the next month in Yemen. Iman (King) Mohammed el-Badr escaped to the mountains on the Saudi Arabian border, where he raised a new army among loyal tribes. Guns, ammunition, and gold were supplied by King Saud, who felt his own kingdom threatened by the Nasserite invasion of the Arabian Peninsula.

When the rebels appealed to Nasser for help, he rushed planes, arms, officers, and troops to the new Yemen republic. The two Yemens plunged into a ruthless civil war that lasted four years, costing Egypt half a million dollars a day and thousands of casualties. Western diplomats viewed the clash as part of a power struggle between Nasser and the Saudis for the rich oil lands of the Arabian Peninsula.

Meanwhile Israel, sensitive to constant UN rebukes for its treatment of the Palestinians, sought to improve its image by making amends to those within its borders. They were granted full political rights, with the right to form parties and vote for their own candidates. Arabic was recognized as an official state language. Palestinians were free to listen to Nasser's anti-Israeli broadcasts from Cairo, and to buy any of fifteen uncensored Arab publications.

Some eighty percent of Arab farmers in Israel were permitted to continue ownership of their land. In border areas where their land was confiscated, compensation was offered. The Israelis saw to it that one hundred twenty mosques within the country's borders were kept repaired and equipped. Arab health benefited from Israel's excellent medical facilities; the Arab infant death rate was lower than in any Arab country.

The Israelis also provided six times as many Arab school-teachers as there had been before the Jewish state was founded. For every Arab child who was sent to school in Saudi Arabia, fifteen were taught in Israel.

But none of these amends softened Palestinian bitterness over Israeli occupation of their country, especially for those who had been forced out of Israel.

All through 1963 the Arab nations grew increasingly dis-united. Saudi Arabia and Egypt were at virtual war in Yemen. Egypt refused to recognize Syria, and broke relations with Jordan. Iraq and Syria were quarreling. The border between Syria and Lebanon was closed. Algeria, Morocco, and Tunisia feuded over border disputes. The Hashemite kingdoms of Jordan and Saudi Arabia were at odds with all radical Arab regimes. And the Palestinians blamed all the Arab nations for doing nothing to get their homeland back. The Arab League was bankrupt — a forum for ventilating bitterness instead of patching up grievances.

National differences were abruptly forgotten, however, when the League convened in January 1964. Arab unity was newly forged by Israel's decision to irrigate the Negev Desert, creating more farmland for immigrants by diverting the headwaters of the River Jordan from the Sea of Galilee. The Arabs decided to thwart this plan by diverting the Jordan's tributaries inside Syria, Lebanon, and Jordan before this water reached Israel. They also agreed to establish a joint Arab military defense under the leadership of Egypt, with the understanding that Nasser would shelve his struggle to revolutionize the Arab world, working for pan-Arabic cooperation instead.

The summit at Cairo also responded to the demands of an impatient younger generation of Palestinians for deeds instead of words. A Palestine Liberation Organization (PLO), along with a guerrilla army made up of Fedayeen commandos, was formed under Ahmed Shukairy. When Shukairy promised in writing not to claim the West Bank for the Palestinians, King Hussein agreed to let him operate from within Jordan. Yet some militant Fedayeen groups that did not consider the PLO aggressive enough continued to function independently.

Nasser's courtship of Washington to obtain arms halted abruptly when the United States insisted that any weaponry given to Egypt must be accompanied by an American military advisory group, to make sure it was not used aggressively. Rejecting this demand as an insult to Egyptian sovereignty, Nasser turned once more to the Soviet Union.

When Moscow agreed to supply him with arms from Communist Czechoslovakia, Nasser released Egyptian Communists from prison as a gesture of reconciliation. The Egyptian Communist party now voted to dissolve and support Nasser. Huge numbers of tanks, self-propelled guns, naval armaments, and jet aircraft began pouring into Egypt. Similar Soviet agreements with Syria and Iraq heavily armed those countries as well. The United States continued equipping the Israeli armed forces.

Egypt and Syria supplied the weapons for commando units of the PLO. In 1965 Yasir Arafat's Al Fatah made over thirty raids into Israel from Jordan, killing a large number of civilians. But five times as many Arabs were killed in attacks on Al Fatah's bases by retaliating Israeli troops.

Habib Bourguiba, president of Tunisia, deplored the bloodshed, blaming Nasser for it. He accused Nasser of refusing to permit peaceful solutions of Middle East problems, of trying to overthrow every Arab state by subversion, of seeking to make himself internationally important to get more aid from both East and West, and of splitting Arab unity.

"Never in their history have the Arabs been so divided," Bourguiba charged in April 1965. "Never have they been killing each other so savagely as since the day when Egypt took upon herself the sacred mission of uniting them."

Enraged, Nasser broke off diplomatic relations.

Syria and Israel continued to clash along their border. As Israeli kibbutzim expanded into Arab farmlands, hundreds of Arab farmers were compelled to flee to the Golan Heights. From here they vented their frustration by firing down on the Israeli settlers working their former farms.

A new revolution in Syria in 1966 paved the way for closer relations with Egypt. Nasser agreed to a special treaty of mutual defense, but made the Syrians pledge to consult him before launching any major military action. Despite the increased arms aid from Moscow, Egypt was in no shape for another war with Israel. The Egyptian army was bogged down in the bloody Yemen struggle. And Nasser's costly social reforms were adding to the strain on the Egyptian economy. Inflation was soaring at the rate of twenty-five percent a year, and Egypt had been forced to default on its international debts.

In November the Israelis, angered by stepped-up Fedayeen raids from both Jordan and Syria, threw planes, tanks, and artillery shells at Jordanian army units. The village of Sammu was almost razed to the ground, with eighteen people killed, fifty-four wounded. The attack was Israel's hint of what Hussein could expect if he did not control the Palestinian commandos.

The scale and ferocity of the raid shocked the West. The UN Security Council passed a vote of condemnation against Israel. Arab passions exploded in violent rioting all over the West Bank. Palestinian civilians demanded arms to defend themselves. Some political observers saw the Israeli blow as a warning to Hussein not to join the Egyptian-Syrian alliance.

Israeli General Itzhak Rabin warned the Syrians in March 1967 that if they continued to permit and aid Palestinian terrorist attacks, it would become necessary "to take action against the country from which these infiltrators come."

On April 7 the Syrians shelled an Israeli kibbutz across the border. The Israeli air force flew over the Syrian artillery and destroyed it. When the Syrians sent up Soviet MIG fighters to oppose them, the Israelis shot down six. Pursuing the rest to Damascus, they staged a victory demonstration in the sky over Syria's capital.

Fearing that the Israelis had decided to overthrow the Damascus government and the guerrilla movement it sheltered, Syria's leaders appealed to their military partner for help. When Nasser failed to respond, he was bitterly assailed as too timid to tangle with the Israelis, bold only in fighting fellow Arabs in the Yemen desert. Calling him soft, the Syrians accused him of "hiding behind the UN troops in Sinai."

Nasser's prestige plummeted in the Arab world.

# 10

# The Six-Day War

SYRIAN FEARS of invasion were heightened when *U.S. News and World Report* revealed that Israeli Premier Levi Eshkol, who had gone to Washington to buy more arms, was told not to waste Israel's money because "the Sixth Fleet is here."

Feeling assured of American support, Eshkol and Rabin uttered sharp public warnings to Syria in May not to risk any further provocations of Israel. Rabin added, "So long as the ardent revolutionists in Damascus have not been overthrown, no government in the Middle East can feel safe."

Trying to force Nasser to come to their rescue, the Syrians showed him Soviet intelligence reports, of doubtful authenticity, indicating that large Israeli troop concentrations were massed on the Syrian border, ready to crush Damascus, then turn and attack Cairo.

Faced with ruin of his leadership if he remained paralyzed, and with disaster if he allowed the crisis to provoke him into an all-out war, Nasser desperately sought to maintain his stature with a show of fierceness that he hoped would intimidate the Israelis and impress his fellow Arabs. If worst came to worst, he reasoned, and war did break out, the Russians could be expected to intervene and force a swift settlement rather than risk the defeat of their Arab clients.

On May 16 he proclaimed a state of emergency, placing all Egyptian military forces "in a complete state of preparedness for war." Syria also mobilized its army into "defensive positions" on the Israeli border. To arouse popular fervor behind him, Nasser sent combat units marching conspicuously through Cairo en route to the Suez front.

"Egypt, with all its resources . . . is ready to plunge into a total war that will be the end of Israel!" he thundered over Radio Cairo. He demanded that UN Secretary General U Thant withdraw the peacekeeping UN Emergency Forces all along the Egyptian-Israeli border, where they had been stationed for ten years by Nasser's consent. As UNEF units moved out, up to eighty thousand Egyptian troops occupied their positions.

Soviet leader Nikita Khrushchev observed later in his memoirs, "It's not at all clear to me why Egypt demanded that U Thant remove the U.N. troops from the border between Egypt and Israel. These forces were a restraining influence on the Israeli aggressors. . . . It's simply incomprehensible to me why Egypt demanded that these forces be removed."

The most likely explanation of Nasser's decision is that it was motivated by Syria's public taunts of Egyptian cowardice in hiding from Israel behind the UN's forces.

On May 19 Egypt's religious leaders were instructed to call for a new *jihad* to regain Palestine for the Arabs. In every Arab city enthusiastic crowds roared for vengeance against Israel for the humiliations of the 1948 War and the occupation of Arab Palestine. On May 27 Arab League members united in a declaration of solidarity with Egypt and Syria.

Ahmed Shukairy spoke for the PLO: "Those native-born Israelis who survive the war will be permitted to remain in the country. But I don't think many will survive." Syria's defense minister, General Hafiz al-Assad, declared, "The time has come to wage the liberation battle."

Reading these threats in the press, and watching TV newscasts of Arab mobs crying for war, Israelis had little doubt that the Arab world was preparing to destroy them. Arabs, in turn, were convinced that the Israelis had determined to overrun the Syrian government, crush the Palestinian movement, then attack Egypt. Nasser was now less a shaper of events than a participant swept up by a storm he was powerless to control. Playing to the Arab gallery, he cried out that the very existence of Israel was "in itself an act of aggression."

At first Western diplomats considered his gambits simply part of a war of nerves, not unlike the ancient Arab practice of having tribal poets win prestige by hurling colorful insults and threats at a rival tribe. Nasser's moves were seen as largely intended for Arab consumption, to reestablish his credibility as leader of the Arab world. The *New York Times* suggested that they were meant to divert Arab attention away from his difficulties in the disastrous Yemen War.

Seeking to calm things down, the Western powers suggested mediation. On May 22 Nasser replied, "The peace talk is heard only when Israel is in danger. But when Arab rights and the rights of the Palestinian people are lost, no one speaks about peace, rights, or anything!"

Washington warned Nasser that his renewed blockade of Israeli shipping in the Gulf of Aqaba was "illegal and potentially dangerous to peace." The Israelis threatened to break the blockade forcibly. The Arab League defended it as "an undeniable act of sovereignty necessitated by Israel's aggressive designs against the Arab states."

Nasser declared on May 26 that if war came, "it will be total and the objective will be to destroy Israel. We feel confident that we can win and are ready now for a war with Israel. . . . We knew that closing the Gulf of Aqaba might mean war with Israel; we will not back down out of our rights." Two days later he warned the Western powers that if any intervened in the Middle East, "there will be no Suez Canal."

Feeling his own kingdom threatened by Israeli mobilization, Hussein flew to Cairo to sign a treaty of common defense with Egypt. Nasser, who until then had been calling for his overthrow, now greeted the king as "dear brother." A few days later Iraq also joined the Arab defense pact.

Arab leaders had once more united around the only issue on which they could all agree — opposition to Israel.

Talking to foreign correspondents on May 30, Nasser indicated that he had been gambling his prestige on the success of a bluff of war. He suggested hopefully, even now, that the crisis be resolved by reviving the Palestine Mixed Armistice Commission to supervise a phased withdrawal of both Egyptian and Israeli forces from their border. He also offered to submit the Gulf of Aqaba dispute to the International Court of Justice. Having achieved his propaganda objectives, he hoped to end the crisis with his honor and prestige restored.

With his best Egyptian troops locked into the civil war in Yemen, he had no illusions about the outcome of a clash with the powerful Israeli army and air force. "I am not in a position to go to war," he acknowledged at Port Said. "I tell you this frankly, and it is not shameful to say it publicly. To go to war without having the sufficient means would be to lead the country and the people to disaster."

On June 2 he told British M.P. Christopher Mayhew that if the Israelis did not attack, "we will leave them alone. We have no intention of attacking Israel." He sent this assurance to Washington as well, offering to negotiate a settlement if Israel would publicly renounce any intention of attacking Syria. Charles Yost, United States special envoy to Cairo, acknowledged, "There does not seem to have been any intention in Cairo to initiate a war."

But other Arab leaders failed to realize that Nasser was trying to lead them back from the brink of war where he had taken them as a diplomatic maneuver. On June 2 Hussein declared, "Our increased cooperation with Egypt and other Arab states . . . will lead us to the erasure of the shame and the liberation of Palestine. This is a cornerstone of our policy."

Hussein's statement, coming from the one Arab leader considered the most moderate voice in the Middle East, shocked the Israeli government. Israeli alarm mounted as Iraq, Kuwait, Saudi Arabia, and Syria threatened to cut off oil shipments to any Western country that aided Israel in the event of war.

Many Israelis now felt that it was hopeless to try to avoid war, and suicidal to wait for the Arabs to strike the first blow.

On June 5, 1967, the Israeli air force suddenly attacked Egyptian, Jordanian, and Syrian airfields. Flying in waves at low level to avoid radar, the attackers destroyed a large part of all Arab air forces on the ground within a few hours, achieving instant mastery of the air over the Middle East.

Tel Aviv issued an untrue communiqué blaming the Arabs for striking the first blow of the war: "Since the early hours of this morning there has been fierce fighting against armoured units and the air force of Egypt which attacked Israel. Our troops went into action to repulse them."

Two hours after the devastating Israeli air attacks, Radio

Amman told Jordanians, "Free citizens, heroic sons of Jordan, the hoped-for moment has arrived. The hour which you longed for is here. Forward to arms, to battle, to new pages of glory! To regain our rights, to smash the aggressor, to revenge!"

Algeria, Iraq, Kuwait, the Sudan, and Yemen joined Jordan, Egypt, and Syria in declaring war on Israel. On the assumption that Washington and London were behind the Israeli attack, violent anti-American and anti-British demonstrations erupted across the Middle East. The Arab oil-producing nations threatened an oil boycott against any Western power helping Israel.

Washington and London quickly announced neutrality, declaring their intention of working toward a peaceful solution of the war. The Soviet Union denounced Israel for aggression.

The Zionist lobby in the United States worked energetically to win funds and supplies for the Israeli cause. American press and public sympathy were largely with Israel, although a small number of Marxists and left-wing radicals blamed "Zionist imperialism" for bringing about the war.

The unchallenged Israeli air force gave close support to Israeli ground forces striking at the Egyptian army in the Gaza Strip. After fierce tank battles on June 6, Gaza fell to the Israelis in one day, along with thousands of Egyptian prisoners and the Palestinian refugee camps.

Radio Cairo broadcast charges that British and American aircraft were aiding the Israeli forces, an accusation denied in London and Washington as "a malicious and mischievous invention." The Arab oil-producing nations nevertheless declared an oil boycott against the United States and Britain.

Egyptian forces reeled back from the Sinai in full retreat, abandoning huge quantities of equipment. The Israeli army fanned out swiftly on June 7, capturing the entire east bank of the Suez Canal. The canal was closed because of shipping sunk within it. Nasser blamed Israeli planes for sinking the ships, but the Israelis accused him. In any event, with the Sinai in their hands, they could now use the Gulf of Aqaba.

Other Israeli forces smashed into Jordan on June 7. After two days of fierce fighting they captured the entire West Bank. The Palestinian refugee camps and the old city of Jerusalem now came under Israeli control.

"We have reunited the torn city, capital of Israel," General Moshe Dayan told his jubilant troops. "We have returned to the most sacred of our shrines, never to part from them again. . . . To our Arab neighbors we offer even now — and with added emphasis at this hour — our hands in peace."

Jordan-Israeli fighting ceased on June 8 when both sides accepted a UN-sponsored cease-fire. That did not prevent the Israelis from launching a final offensive next day against Syria. The Syrians accused them of using napalm against villages as well as military positions, leveling the villages to the ground. A fourth of the population of the Golan Heights was driven off by the fighting. Syrian resistance collapsed, and on June 11 the UN established a cease-fire in place.

In six days the Arabs had sustained a humiliating defeat of staggering proportions, losing the Sinai, Jerusalem, the West Bank, the Gaza Strip, and the Golan Heights. The Egyptians had suffered 25,000 casualties, the Jordanians almost 3,000, Syria 2,000, while Israel reported 759 men killed. The Israelis had demonstrated that the Arabs were no match for a highly motivated modern army, well trained, well led, and skillfully coordinated by expert military strategists.

From China both Mao Tse-tung and Chou En-lai wrote to Nasser urging him to fight on by breaking up the Egyptian army into guerrilla units that would lose themselves in the population and keep the Israelis under commando attacks. Nasser replied that Egypt had lost its army, and anyhow, to try to fight on would merely give the Israelis an opportunity to destroy Egypt piecemeal. Besides, he added, Sinai was a desert: "We cannot conduct a people's liberation war in Sinai because there are no people there."

It seemed inevitable that the stunning defeat of the Six-Day War would finish the career of the Arab leader identified with it. Nasser had clearly overplayed his hand by hurling reckless threats at the strongest nation in the Middle East, exposing the Arab countries and their armies to total disaster.

Acknowledging his responsibility, Nasser told the Egyptian people in a June 9 broadcast that he intended to resign. The Arab cause had suffered "a grave setback," he admitted, at the hands of a nation that had struck "a stronger blow than we expected."

Already stunned by the trauma of defeat, the Egyptians were further dismayed at the thought of losing their leader. Even if he had failed them on the battlefield, Nasser was still the hero who had rid them of King Farouk, ended the British occupation, given Egypt control of the Suez Canal, built the Aswan Dam, introduced land reform, built many factories and schools, and improved the lot of the average worker and peasant. And was not Nasser the chief architect of Arab nationalism?

Hundreds of thousands of Egyptians poured into the streets of Cairo, weeping and shouting, "Nasser, Nasser don't leave us — we need you!" The whole country seemed to be in mourning. Tens of thousands marched on the National Assembly, threatening to kill any deputies who accepted Nasser's resignation. The assembly quickly asked him to reconsider and stay on as the only leader with unanimous support.

There was great rejoicing when Nasser, genuinely touched by the depth of popular feeling for him, consented "in view of the people's determination to refuse my resignation." Once more, as after the Suez War, he demonstrated in defeat a unique ability to unite the Arab people behind him.

The Six-Day War had made it painfully clear that the Arab world lacked the ability to utilize the techniques and technology of modern warfare. But the impression created in the Western press that Arab soldiers had turned tail and fled in terror before "little Israel" was inaccurate. Most observers agreed that they had actually demonstrated impressive courage against an awesomely efficient Israeli war machine.

The war in 1967 tripled the territory held by the Israelis and brought them important new sources of revenue. Jerusalem would bring in tourist dollars; there was oil in the Sinai desert; and the West Bank of the Jordan River was rich agricultural country.

The Arab nations were too shocked and divided to develop any new strategy for coping with an enlarged and more powerful Israel. Egypt and Jordan now felt it necessary to end all talk of "liquidating" Israel, and perhaps reach a deal with the Israelis based on their withdrawal from occupied territory. Syria, rejecting all political compromise as futile, called instead for renewing the struggle through guerrilla warfare.

All Arab leaders felt bitter toward the Western press for what they considered biased reporting of the war. They objected to the constant comparison of Israel to a tiny, underdog David slaying a huge Arab Goliath. The world had not been informed, the Arabs complained, that the effective troop strength of all Arab forces in 1967 had been no more than 285,000, scattered around the Middle East, while Israel had had 300,000 troops concentrated under one central command.

The Western press had also portrayed Nasser as a kind of Middle East Hitler, pressing a genocidal war on the Jews of Israel. In Arab eyes, this was a Western ploy to transfer guilt for Europe's persecution of the Jews onto the Arabs.

"I have never been anti-Semitic on a personal level," Nasser vowed to a British interviewer. "It is very difficult for a thinking

Egyptian to be so. We have so many basic links—after all, Moses himself was an Egyptian. My feelings and actions against Israel later were inspired solely by the Israelis' actions as a state."

There was also resentment of the Western press for confusing the issue of who had actually begun the war. But United States Senator Ernest Gruening replied, "Whether the Israelis struck first is only of academic interest. When an individual points a loaded gun at you and states repeatedly that he is going to kill you, the law provides and common sense dictates that you do not wait until he shoots you before taking reasonable measures to resist the aggression. The situation in the Middle East on June 5, 1967, was as simple as that."

Many foreign affairs experts considered the Six-Day War a "chain reaction conflict," one that neither side had really wanted or planned, but that J. Bowyer Bell of the Harvard Center for International Affairs characterized as the result of a "snowballing process of miscalculation."

The Israelis had been misled by Nasser's belligerent public propaganda designed to impress the Arab world, while privately he took a moderate and rational view. The Arabs had been misled into believing that Israel was planning to launch a new war against them with American and British support, and that a show of force and bluster could prevent the attack. Nasser had also erred in thinking that he could go to the brink of war, and then be bought off with diplomatic gains.

Now the worst fears of the Arabs had been realized. The new Israeli conquests had swept an additional one million Arabs under Israeli control. Many were refugees who had been exiled by the 1948 War. A new flight of panic-stricken Arabs began into Jordan, Syria, and Lebanon, encouraged by Israeli military authorities who did not want responsibility for them, and feared an Arab "fifth column" within the new borders.

Many Arabs were forced out of their homes and villages, while others fled to escape internment in camps or jails.

On the CBS program *Face the Nation,* General Moshe Dayan was asked about Israel's ability to absorb the Arab population in the occupied territories. He replied, "Economically we can; but I think that is not in accord with our aims in the future. It would turn Israel into either a bi-national or poly-Arab-Jewish state instead of the Jewish state, and we want to have a Jewish state. We can absorb them, but then it won't be the same country."

The Arabs charged the Israelis with uprooting four hundred thousand Palestinians from their homes in Gaza and the West Bank, and over one hundred thousand Palestinians and Syrians in the Kuneitra area. In Jerusalem's Moroccan quarter, four hundred Arab families had been given just three hours to evacuate their homes. In three West Bank villages, all the people were ordered to leave, after which the villages had been totally destroyed by dynamite.

A French missionary, Sister Marie-Therese, noted, "Alone in a deathly silence donkeys wandered about the ruins. Here and there a crushed piece of furniture or a torn pillow stuck out of the mass of plaster, stones and concrete." One Arab mother who returned to her village gaped at the space where the homes had been only hours earlier. "Just like a dream," she said. "It's as if we've never been there."

London *Times* correspondents Ian Gilmour and Dennis Walters reported from the West Bank on psychological tactics used by the Israelis to drive Arabs out of the occupied territory:

"At one village . . . after the leading Arab was seen talking to the Israel commander, a rumour suddenly spread that anybody remaining in the village one hour later would be killed. All the inhabitants left, and, by a fortunate coincidence, they found just outside the village buses provided to transport them to the River Jordan. . . . Soldiers knock at houses a number of times each night; after a bit the children are reduced to nervous wrecks and the family decides to leave. . . . We are convinced that after the initial panic the bulk of the refugees have been and still are being forced out."

Gilmore and Walters contradicted a Western report that Israel had agreed to the return of refugees and was repatriating them. "Nothing could be further from the truth," they wrote. "Certainly on one day, in front of television cameras, 144 were allowed to return over the Allenby Bridge. Unfortunately, there was no television to record that over other bridges on that same day, more than three times that figure were going in the other direction. . . . The sad traffic of exodus has continued at a rate of about 1,000 a day."

Some Israelis themselves were upset by their government's treatment of the Palestinians. One Israeli soldier sent to a refugee camp to quell rioting confessed that he felt "like a Gestapo man. . . . I thought of home, I thought of my parents being led away."

Dr. Israel Shahak, a Polish Jew who had spent his childhood in the Warsaw Ghetto and the Nazi concentration camp at Belsen, organized the Israeli League for Human and Civil Rights. He published the Shahak Report enumerating the Arab villages destroyed by Israel. The Israeli government charged Dr. Shahak and the league with pro-Arab bias because they accepted Arab members.

Moscow's *Izvestia* accused Israeli soldiers of looting and committing atrocities. *Time* magazine dismissed the charges as largely Communist propaganda, but then quoted Moshe Dayan's admission, "An army of regulars and reservists of various ages and psychological drives cannot be perfect."

In a June 26 address to the UN, King Hussein accused the Israeli army of using napalm and fragmentation bombs. He also charged them with "inhuman and indecent treatment of prisoners-of-war, with mutilating and destroying Jordanian and other Arab towns and villages and driving the inhabitants from their homes." If the UN failed to compel Israel to return to its former borders, he warned, "the battle which began on June 5 will . . . become only a battle in what will be a long war."

Two days later Israel formally annexed Jerusalem, despite pleas from the West that this would prejudice any chances of a peace settlement. The UN General Assembly passed a resolution declaring the annexation invalid.

On August 8 Jordan's finance minister, Abdel Wahab Majali, urged Palestinians who had fled captured territory to return. "Every refugee should return to help his brothers to continue their political action," he declared, "and remain a thorn in the flesh of the aggressor until the crisis has been solved."

The war had proved such a financial disaster for both Jordan and Egypt that their oil-wealthy neighbors, Kuwait, Saudi Arabia, and Libya, agreed at a Khartoum conference called at the end of August to provide annual subsidies to help them recover from the costly debacle. Nasser agreed with relief to a Saudi proposal that they both disengage from the war in Yemen.

The Arab nations now decided to lift the oil embargo against the Western powers and seek a peaceful political settlement with Israel, with the help of the UN, provided this could be done through indirect negotiations without formal recognition of the Israeli state. But first Israel would have to agree to withdraw to its previous borders.

Although the Khartoum conference represented a victory for the moderate Arab faction, Israel viewed its proposals as offering only a hard-line policy — "no peace, no negotiations, no recognition." The Israeli reply: "No soap."

After visiting the occupied territories, the London *Times* foreign editor, C. Hodgkins, reported in October that the Israelis continued to find the presence of the Arabs they had overrun "inconvenient." He explained, "As it would be much simpler if these were not there, every effort is being made to persuade them to go. The most important ones to be got rid of are those with education and authority."

But the Arabs were equally determined that the Palestinians must be allowed to remain where they were. Justice demanded it; honor required it. Former British Foreign Minister Anthony Nutting declared that after the Six-Day War he often heard Arabs say in effect, "It took us two hundred years to get rid of the Crusaders. All right! If Israel will make no terms, if Israel will make no amends to the Palestine people, we will wait two hundred years and we will get rid of them in the end as we got rid of the Crusaders, another European incursion, another Western beachhead upon our shores."

Hussein offered the Israeli government a peaceful settlement of their differences in the fall of 1967. "Our offer," he declared, "would mean that we recognize the right of all to live in peace and security." Speaking officially for Egypt, Dr. Mohammed H. al-Zayyat declared that his government was prepared to guarantee "the right of Israel to exist."

The Israelis rejected both overtures because of a condition requiring them to give back the captured territories.

On November 22, 1967, the UN Security Council adopted an important measure. Resolution 242 declared the "inadmissibility of the acquisition of territory by war." Israel was called upon to evacuate the West Bank of Jordan, the Golan Heights of Syria, and the Sinai peninsula of Egypt.

In the interests of a just and lasting peace, it required an end to all territorial claims; recognition of the sovereignty of each nation; the right of each nation to be secure from threats or acts of force; freedom of navigation through international waterways; a "just settlement of the refugee problem"; demilitarized buffer zones to assure peace; and appointment of a special UN representative who would see to it that these arrangements were complied with properly.

Egypt and Jordan accepted the terms of Resolution 242. Syria, the PLO, and other Palestinian organizations condemned it as a "sellout" because it assured Israel of recognition as a sovereign state, while relegating the Palestinians to a dubious future as "refugees."

When UN Ambassador Gunnar Jarring undertook to implement Resolution 242, the Israelis demanded face-to-face negotiations with the Arabs, which would imply Arab recognition. They also refused to withdraw from any occupied territories before the Arabs signed binding peace agreements.

Hussein and Nasser made it clear to Jarring that their acceptance of Resolution 242 depended upon Israel's withdrawal before any negotiations began. Deadlock.

The chances for a settlement grew dimmer every day as the Israelis continued expropriating Arab-owned land. Expelling Arabs and bulldozing villages, they founded quasi-military settlements in the West Bank, Gaza, and Golan Heights.

The Fedayeen, now scorning Nasser as a compromiser and appeaser, decided to take the struggle against Israel increasingly into their own hands. During November and December 1967, Arab commando squads began blowing up Israeli installations. On December 21 Israel rounded up fifty-six suspects of a "major terrorist network," and announced that three hundred "marauders" had been captured and fifty killed since the end of the Six-Day War.

In the West Bank, Israeli emergency regulations punished swiftly and drastically any Arab involved with the Fedayeen. Anyone who helped them was subject to arrest and imprisonment, and his house was demolished. Many uninvolved Palestinians were unhappy at being caught in the cross fire between the Israelis and the guerrillas. Some sought to stave off trouble by secretly informing Israeli security forces as to the hiding places of PLO commandos.

Arab unity was not only a rare commodity among Arab leaders; it was hard to come by among the people themselves.

# 11

# The Arabs Strike Back

"ARABS IN ISRAEL are the fifth column, either voluntarily or under coercion," declared the Israeli Ministry of Public Education. By a search-and-destroy policy, Israeli security forces sought to keep the Fedayeen off balance, preventing them from organizing a strong network of popular support such as Mao, Castro, and Ho Chi Minh had won for their revolutionary movements. The Fedayeen kept up raids from Jordan.

Israeli planes bombed and shelled the east bank in retaliation. Jordan accused them of deliberately attacking civilian targets, including refugee camps, in an attempt to "sever all links between the two banks of the river . . . [and] break down the people's will to resist."

The Israelis regarded the efforts of the Fedayeen as more of a nuisance than a real threat — mine-laying, sniping, a few ambushes, firing across the border. Nevertheless, on March 21, 1968, a column of up to ten thousand Israelis, supported by tanks and air strikes, attacked the Jordanian village of Karameh, the commando base of Al Fatah.

Instead of fading away, the Fedayeen this time fought back in hand-to-hand combat, supported by the Jordanian army. The battle raged for fifteen hours, until many of the Fedayeen had been killed or captured and the village largely destroyed. The Arabs still continued fierce resistance from hillsides above the village, finally compelling the Israelis to withdraw without their dead and damaged tanks.

Trophies of the battle of Karameh were triumphantly paraded through Amman and shown on TV all over the Middle East, offering Arabs a badly needed morale booster. Karameh proved that the Israelis weren't supermen after all, and that well-led Arab forces could stand up to their military power.

Yasir Arafat's prestige soared, and eager recruits flooded into Al Fatah. Hussein lodged a complaint with the UN Security Council against Israel, which was once more censured for an act of aggression.

But the Israeli government had determined upon a hard line toward the Arabs. The new regime in Jerusalem made it difficult for Arabs to get work in the city, imposed new taxes and confiscated the property of those who could not pay them, and curbed Arab exports — measures the Arabs protested were intended to drive them out of the Holy City.

Some Israelis worried that such severe treatment made violent resistance by the commandos inevitable. Ben-Gurion himself admitted privately that if he were a young Arab, he, too, might also join the Fedayeen.

In May 1968 the Palestinians sought to unify their ranks through a national council that would function as a rudimentary government-in-exile. Al Fatah, led by Arafat, won a third of the seats. Smaller rival groups included the Popular Front for the Liberation of Palestine (PFLP) under Dr. George Habash of Lebanon; the Popular Democratic Front for the Liberation of Palestine (PDFLP) under Nayef Awatmeh, a Jordanian Christian; and the Arab Nationalist Movement (ANM), a pan-Arab group.

But Arab rivalries were too strong, and the struggle for leadership of the Palestine National Council resulted in all factions continuing to act independently.

Funds for the Palestinians came from the oil-rich sheikhs of Kuwait, Libya, and especially Saudi Arabia, where Ibn Saud's son Faisal was now on the throne. Faisal was determined upon the liberation of Arab Jerusalem, hoping to pray in the Al Aqsa mosque before he died. Thus money from the most ultraconservative monarchy in the Arab world found its way to the revolutionary Al Fatah, which dominated the Fedayeen movement.

In Fedayeen eyes, the chief foreign enemy of the Arabs was the United States, because of its arming of Israel and indifference to Palestinian suffering. Israel was considered an "American colony," intended to keep the Arab nations in economic and political subjection to the West. Washington was blamed for the pro-Israeli viewpoint of the American press, and for Israel's refusal to give up conquered territory.

Late in the summer of 1968 Arafat succeeded in persuading Lebanese Premier Abdullah Yaffi to allow a small force of sixty Fedayeen to establish secret headquarters in southeast Lebanon. They quickly expanded into a guerrilla army of many thousands, which began raiding northeast Israel, while the Fedayeen based in Jordan stepped up attacks from the southeast.

By the end of 1968 the Fedayeen in Jordan had grown into a political force powerful enough to represent a threat to the authority of King Hussein, who found himself unable to control them. Within the refugee camps the Fedayeen developed a "state within a state," with their own army, finances, social services, and foreign diplomacy.

Some Fedayeen leaders were arrested in November for violating Jordanian law. After a heated confrontation, the Palestinians and Hussein's ministers worked out an uneasy accommodation under which the Fedayeen were granted a limited amount of autonomy. But both sides knew that if the Palestinians failed to get their homeland back, there was bound to be a showdown in Jordan with the government over their status.

As part of its overseas operations against Israel, Habash's PFLP sent commandos from Lebanon to attack an El Al aircraft at Athens Airport. The Israelis retaliated on December 29, 1968, with a massive airborne raid against Beirut International Airport, blowing up thirteen airliners on the ground.

Despite severe punishment by Israel for harboring the Fedayeen, neither Lebanon nor Jordan dared attempt to curb the Palestinians because their crusade against Israel commanded the support of the whole Arab world.

Traveling around the Middle East in a flowing headdress and dark glasses, Arafat was welcomed by Arab leaders as virtual head of a Palestine government-in-exile. As chief spokesman for the Palestinian cause, he warned, "Israel . . . will never be safe as long as she refuses to recognize the rights of the Palestinian people." Disclaiming any intention of driving the Jews out of Israel, he insisted that Jews and Arabs could live peacefully together in one unified, nonsectarian, and democratic state of Palestine.

George Habash criticized Al Fatah's raids on Israel as too ineffectual and limited a strategy to have any real impact. He advocated acts of terrorism on a larger stage outside the Middle East, compelling the world to take notice of the Palestinian cause, even if only with a sense of outrage.

Habash sent well-dressed young men and women of the PFLP to Europe to commit dramatic acts of political violence. "We want the world to know that the whole Palestinian community, women and children as well as men, is imbued with revolutionary fervor," he explained. "And we want it to know that they are modern people and that they are civilized."

Lack of world sympathy, Habash believed, stemmed from a poor image of the Arab as either a primitive desert Bedouin or an illiterate refugee, in contrast to the image of the Israeli as a modern, brave, resourceful, and intelligent pioneer.

Unless a specific Fedayeen organization claimed credit for a terrorist act, it was not easy to determine which group was responsible. In March 1969 a bomb exploded in the cafeteria of Jerusalem's Hebrew University, where one hundred seventy Arab students were enrolled — perhaps for that reason.

"Most of us, including myself, are deeply opposed to any kind of sabotage acts whatsoever, and we condemn them," declared Ahmed Marsalha, an Arab student of sociology. "My Jewish friends from before the explosion have, I believe, remained my friends and will remain so. We Israeli Arabs have lived with the Jews for twenty years, we speak the same language, see the same films, read the same books and eat the same food. The only thing that sets me apart from my Jewish student friends is that I tune in from time to time to the Arab radio stations."

Israeli university officials decided against imposing any restrictions on its Arab students because of the bombing.

In September 1969 the royalist Arab nations were upset when a coup in Libya led by a radical young officer, Muammur al Qaddafi, deposed King Indris. Qaddafi proclaimed Libya a socialist republic. The news reached Nasser during a meeting with King Hussein. Without thinking, Nasser exclaimed,

"Wonderful — another Arab king overthrown!" Hussein later said grimly, "That scene will be forever engraved in my memory."

Dramatic acts of terrorism by the PFLP forced Arafat to take Al Fatah further to the left, in order not to lose leadership of the Palestinian movement to Habash. Al Fatah reportedly developed a new terrorist branch called "Black September," which was soon to make the violence of the PFLP pale by comparison.

In the view of Henry Kissinger, then foreign policy advisor to President Richard M. Nixon, the Arabs had grown desperate, losing their "sense of dignity" because of "living at the mercy" of the Israelis. This was why, in frustration, they had turned to the Communist world for help in reclaiming Palestine. That, in turn, posed problems for the United States, which feared Communist influence in the Middle East as a threat to the oil fields the West depended upon to keep its industrial economy afloat. Kissinger's policy was to give financial and military aid to the conservative and moderate Arab regimes, strengthening them against the Arab revolutionaries.

King Hussein, who received such aid, sought to keep anti-Israeli activities in Jordan to a minimum level, commensurate with his obligations as a member of the Arab League. This policy added to his unpopularity with Palestinian commandos, who were determined to overthrow him. Hussein, in turn, steeled himself for a decision that he knew would make him a target for bitter criticism in the Arab world — using his Arab Legion to drive the Fedayeen out of Jordan.

In June 1970 the PFLP took over the two largest hotels in Amman, holding eighty foreigners hostage to guarantee that the Arab Legion would not attack Fedayeen headquarters in the refugee camps. Armed PFLP commandos rode jauntily around

Amman in jeeps like an army of occupation, while Jordanian army officers fumed in rage at orders tying their hands.

Seeking to prevent bloody civil war, Hussein made several new concessions to the Fedayeen, which only weakened his authority without winning their allegiance. Now he determined to crush them on the next plausible pretext.

That opportunity came in September when the PFLP hijacked four Western commercial jet airliners, grounding them in Jordan. Unleashing the Arab Legion against the Palestinians, Hussein killed more of them than the Israelis had in the Six-Day War, and drove huge numbers to flight. On September 27, 1970, Nasser ended the savage fighting by reconciling Hussein and Arafat. One day later he died of a heart attack.

Egyptians crowded into the streets in wild demonstrations of grief, many crying out their refusal to believe the news: "Nasser is *not* dead!" Most of the Arab world keenly felt the loss of the leader who had been their most powerful symbol of pan-Arab nationalism, independence from foreign powers, modernization, and social justice. Some Arab critics faulted him for having been inconsistent, conspiratorial, and dictatorial, and for having brought about the disastrous Six-Day War.

Nasser's successor was his longtime lieutenant, Anwar Sadat, a mild-looking man who lacked Nasser's charisma and mystique, but who emerged as a resourceful, pragmatic leader more willing to face realities than Nasser had been.

Sadat offered to reopen the Suez Canal and guarantee the right of Israeli shipping through the Gulf of Aqaba, if Israel withdrew some of its troops from the Sinai peninsula and freed the occupied east bank of the canal. Israel refused.

Life for Palestinians on the Israeli-occupied West Bank of Jordan grew increasingly difficult. West Bankers complained that whatever they did was dangerous. If they obeyed the

Fedayeen and shot an Israeli, Israeli police would put them in prison for life. If instead they took jobs under the Israelis, their lives were endangered as "collaborators."

In mid-1971 three grenades were hurled at Israeli targets on the main street of Nablus without exploding. A wry West Bank joke explained that the Fedayeen had paid a Palestinian to throw the grenades, while the Israelis had paid him not to pull the pins out when he did.

The tragic existence of Palestinians forced to live in refugee camps continued unabated. "Regardless of what standard we adopt — education, health, nutrition, housing — life in the camps is an affront to elementary humanity," observed sociologist Stephen A. Garrett of the Monterey Institute of Foreign Studies. "After seeing the squalor of a camp outside Sidon in southern Lebanon, my immediate reaction was to be astonished not that there was so much political fanaticism among the Palestinians but that there was so little. . . . The refugee camps are fertile soil for the politics of violence."

Palestinian leaders persistently accused the Israelis of torturing captured Fedayeen for information. When British foreign correspondent David Pryce-Jones probed these charges, an Israeli general told him, "It depends upon what you mean by torture. Nine out of the ten guerrillas we capture are so frightened that they tell us everything they know. As for the one who doesn't talk, you have only to do like this — ." And he raised his hands in a gesture of face-slapping.

Whether or not more severe mistreatment was involved, the Israelis were not loath to have the Arabs believe the torture stories, thus inducing captured Fedayeen to talk out of fear. But the Israelis steadfastly denied to correspondents that they used torture in the sense that the world understood it.

The PFLP and Black September persisted in acts of terrorism abroad despite the fact that world opinion, rather than mobilizing on their behalf, was horrified at the skyjackings, the assassinations and kidnappings of officials, the murders at the Olympics, the airport massacres, the letter bombs.

Terror tactics divided the Arabs themselves along class lines. The crusade for Palestine involved a struggle between conservative and moderate Arab regimes on one hand, and revolutionary regimes on the other. The more radical the regime, the more it supported Fedayeen acts of terrorism.

Palestinian pressures, plus the desire of Egypt and Syria to get back their lost territories, led to Arab plans for a surprise attack on Israel. The date chosen had special significance. October 6, 1973, was Yom Kippur, the holiest day in the Jewish calendar, when the Israelis could be expected to be preoccupied with religious celebrations. It was also the anniversary of the ancient battle of Badr, which had won Mohammed entry into Mecca, beginning the spread of Islam.

The Yom Kippur War represented a gamble by Anwar Sadat that he could regain control of the Suez Canal, whose lost revenues were sorely needed by Egypt, as well as the Abu Rudeis oil field in the Sinai. If Israel could be caught by surprise, and captured ground held before the Israelis could counterattack, Sadat counted on big power intervention to stop the fighting, leaving him in control of reconquered territory, with recognition as the new leader of a reunited Arab world. From that position of strength, he could then negotiate a final settlement with Israel.

On October 5 Egyptian forces crossed the Suez Canal at five points, while the Syrian army attacked two sectors of the Golan Heights. In six days the Egyptian army established a bridgehead of sixty thousand men in the Sinai desert, their advance protected by new Soviet antiaircraft missiles that kept the Israeli air force from hurling them back.

Caught off guard, Israel lost ground on both fronts. Iraq and Jordan sent forces to join the attack on the Syrian front. When the Israelis finally mounted a counterattack, they drove hard into Syria until they were only eighteen miles from Damascus. Another Israeli force in the west encircled the Egyptians in the Sinai, then crossed the Suez Canal to attack Egyptian tanks, artillery, and missile sites on the West Bank.

By October 24 the Israelis had isolated the city of Suez, and cut off the Egyptian Third Army in the Sinai. Protesting that this action had come after a UN Security Council resolution calling for a cease-fire in place, Sadat demanded that the Israelis retreat to their position held two days earlier. The Israelis refused, facing the surrounded Egyptian Third Army with the option of surrender or starvation.

The Yom Kippur War was no clear-cut victory for either side, both sides suffering heavy losses in troops and war matériel. But its outcome delighted the Arab world and shocked the West, which had not believed the Egyptian army capable of standing up to Israeli military power. Sadat's advance into the Sinai gave Arabs everywhere a new sense of pride and self-confidence. The stigma of inferiority had finally been erased, they felt, compelling Israel and the West to respect the courage and ability of Arabic fighting forces.

Israelis were stunned, angrily blaming leaders who had left the country unprepared for the surprise Arab attack.

Henry Kissinger, now United States secretary of state, undertook a series of "shuttle diplomacy" flights between Cairo and Tel Aviv, seeking to transform a shaky UN cease-fire into a peace agreement. He counted on Saudi Arabia's Faisal to keep most Arab leaders in line behind an American policy of step-by-step negotiations between Israel and the Arabs. Faisal's vast oil revenues, which provided subsidies for some Arab nations, made him a powerful factor in the Arab world.

To improve the chances for a lasting Middle East settlement, Kissinger sought to better American relations with Egypt. His efforts were welcomed by Sadat, who asked only that Washington display a more evenhanded policy toward the Arabs. The Egypt of Sadat was now far less radical than it had been under Nasser, and far less anti-American.

Sadat looked to Washington for the economic help Egypt sorely needed, help that he felt was much more likely to be forthcoming from the Americans than from the Russians. Relations between Egypt and the Soviet Union grew chilly.

At an Arab summit in Rabat in October 1974, the Palestine Liberation Organization, now recognized as sole representative of the Palestinians with Yasir Arafat as their spokesman, was authorized to form an official government-in-exile, and to prepare for negotiations with Israel.

But Israeli Prime Minister Itzhak Rabin declared, "There are no negotiations with terrorist organizations." Extremists within the PLO likewise opposed any diplomatic solution.

Washington found Sadat eager for an accord with Israel because of growing social unrest in Egypt. In January 1975 workers and students rioted in Cairo, protesting soaring living costs and shortages of basic commodities. Stoning buses and store windows, one rioter shouted sardonically, "Oh, hero of the Suez Canal crossing, where is our breakfast?"

An accord with Israel would permit Sadat to reopen the canal, and also pave the way for foreign multinational corporations that had plans for opening industrial plants in the canal zone. They were reluctant to make any start in this direction until they could be assured that their investments would not be jeopardized by another war in the Sinai.

Something of a furor broke out in the American press when a congressional hearing disclosed that many American corporations were refusing to do business with Israel, to avoid being put on an Arab blacklist maintained by Saudi Arabia to punish firms that did business with Israel by not buying from them.

Faisal's brother, Khalid ibn Abdel Aziz, who succeeded him as king of Saudi Arabia after Faisal's assassination in March 1975, had a different interpretation of why Israel was losing American support. "I see that the Zionist influence is being faced for the first time with a clear U.S. resistance," he declared, "accompanied by a tendency to contact the Arabs and understand their viewpoints. We should encourage this tendency and make it easier for the Americans to understand the facts."

Arab spokesmen intensified their efforts in the UN.

Kissinger's shuttle diplomacy bore fruit. Israel agreed to withdraw its forces to fortified passes in the Sinai fourteen miles back from the canal, allowing Egyptian troops to flank both banks of the canal, and to turn over the Abu Rudeis oil field to Sadat. Sadat agreed to let Israeli cargoes through the canal, and gave an off-the-record assurance of no further belligerence against Israel.

For Kissinger's diplomatic triumph, however, both sides made him pay an American price. He was expected to get Congress to agree to station two hundred American technicians in the buffer zone in the Sinai between the two armies manned by the UN. They were wanted to man radar warning devices to prevent surprise attacks by either side, but more importantly as an earnest of American involvement in keeping the peace.

As rewards for being reasonable, Egypt and Israel also expected American grants of economic and military aid.

Although snags developed in spelling out the precise terms of the proposed peace agreement, Sadat showed his confidence in a final settlement by announcing on April 7 that he would reopen the Suez Canal in June. This news dismayed Syria and the PLO, indicating that Sadat had hung up his guns. Sadat angered them further by agreeing to meet President Gerald Ford in Austria to discuss remaining differences.

"Everyone knows that all the cards in this game are in the

hands of the United States," Sadat told Dutch journalists. "I am going to listen to what he has to say."

In preparation for this meeting, Sadat sought to line up support for a negotiated Middle East settlement by touring the Arab world. The Iraqis gave him a tumultuous welcome. King Khalid of Saudi Arabia promised to recognize Israel if it withdrew from all Arab territories taken subsequent to the Six-Day War. Syria reluctantly agreed not to insist upon Israeli withdrawal from the Golan Heights as a precondition for further Israeli-Egyptian negotiations. And Sadat won the support of Hussein in the first journey to Jordan ever undertaken by an Egyptian leader.

"Today we in Jordan, as well as in Egypt and Syria, are ready, even eager, to make peace," Hussein declared during a visit to the United States in May.

On June 5 Sadat reopened the Suez Canal with colorful ceremonies, leading a procession of ships that sailed through the waterway for the first time in eight years. "This is one of the happiest days of my life," he declared. Crowds along the banks roared, "Sadat! Sadat!" His cup of delight ran over when Saudi Arabia promised to erect a whole new metropolis, Faisal City, to house fifty thousand Egyptians along the canal.

Reassured by this clear signal that Sadat had pledged Egypt to peace with Israel, the Israelis pulled their forces eighteen miles back from the Suez front, and withdrew all artillery within shelling range of the waterway.

Just when hopes soared for peace in the Middle East, savage fighting broke out in Lebanon. There was bad blood between the private militia of the Christian Phalange party and the Moslem PLO guerrilla forces stationed in Beirut. There were other grievances besides religious hatred. The Phalange blamed the PLO for bringing Israeli attacks on Lebanon by their raids into Israel. The Moslems resented the Christian Arabs' control of the government and the economy.

In many respects the fighting between the two groups represented an Arab class struggle for control of the country.

"They can kill our people and rocket our refugee camps," declared one Palestinian bitterly. "But if they want a showdown we can destroy their property — which is what hurts the Phalangists most."

The fighting in Lebanon raged to the level of civil war, continuing into 1976. Dozens of attempts at cease-fires broke down as the fighting destroyed much of the business and tourist district of Beirut, jeopardizing the city's position as the international trade capital of the Middle East. Most foreign companies and embassies packed and left.

Anti-Palestinian feeling was less open, but nonetheless present, in other Arab countries besides Lebanon, despite lip service paid to the Palestinian cause. They regarded the Palestinians as "troublemakers," stumbling blocks to the negotiated peace settlement with Israel that many Arab leaders felt was essential. Hussein began easing Palestinians out of his civil service and army as quickly as he could find qualified Jordanians to replace them. Even Syria, which provided the PLO with arms, training, and logistic support, planted secret police agents in the refugee camps to keep a distrustful eye on the Fedayeen.

Determined to block all moves toward a peace that left their homeland in Israeli hands, militant Fedayeen leaders received funds and encouragement from oil-rich Libya's Qaddafi. Denouncing Sadat, they launched an intensified "no peace with Israel" campaign. Bombs exploded in Tel Aviv's Savoy Hotel, killing eighteen guests, and in Jerusalem's Zion Square, killing thirteen shoppers and wounding seventy-two more.

Egyptian intelligence reported that Qaddafi had offered the PFLP sixteen million dollars to assassinate Sadat, and that Habash had agreed. Sadat labeled Qaddafi "100 percent sick and possessed by the devil." The two leaders exchanged scathing sallies, splitting the unity of the Arab world still further.

When Kissinger finally hammered out a new interim Sinai peace agreement acceptable to both Egypt and Israel, pending endorsement by the American Congress, suspicion of it was widespread in both Middle East camps. Israeli critics charged that it was an attempt to give President Gerald Ford the appearance of a diplomatic triumph to exploit in his campaign for election in 1976.

When Kissinger visited Jerusalem, angry Israeli crowds hurled eggs and shouted, "Kissinger, go home!" One furious Israeli shouted, "What's in the agreement for Israel?" Kissinger replied, "Peace and security. A future for your country."

The Palestinians were convinced that Sadat was selling out the Arab cause for American economic help. Fedayeen terrorists seized the Egyptian embassy in Madrid, took the ambassador hostage, and demanded that Sadat renounce the Sinai pact.

"There are those who think they can pressure us into changing our path," he replied. "We say no. Nothing of the sort will ever happen." The terrorists finally agreed to release the ambassador in return for being allowed to escape.

"This American solution cannot, cannot, cannot take place," thundered Yasir Arafat. "We will liberate Palestine with our blood, bodies and souls!"

The Sinai pact also ran into opposition from Congress, which fretted over the requirement that two hundred American technicians be placed between the two Middle East armies. Wasn't this kind of small "technical" assistance exactly the way the disastrous American involvement in the Vietnam War had begun? There was also reluctance to spend over three billion dollars in aid, in a time of recession, to "buy" peace from both sides.

Kissinger pleaded, "You cannot understand this agreement unless you recognize the alternative, and the alternative is war by Christmas." He argued that only such step-by-step diplomacy, winning one agreement at a time, could hope to succeed, since attempting a total solution to the complicated Middle East problem would be a long, possibly hopeless, task.

To pacify Syria, Sadat made it clear that the Sinai pact was predicated on an American commitment to arrange a similar settlement between Syria and Israel. But with Egypt neutralized as a threat, Israel felt less need to make any concessions to Syria's demand for a return of the Golan Heights.

Since many Fedayeen attacks had been launched against Israeli kibbutz border settlements from the Heights, Israel declared its need to hold this outpost as a "buffer zone." Syria labeled this claim a pretext, since Israelis had begun settling on the Heights, transforming it from a buffer zone to occupied territory, making new clashes inevitable.

In November 1975 Sadat came to the United States on a goodwill tour, addressing a joint session of Congress to appeal for passage of the Sinai pact. Highly visible on TV, he made a distinctly favorable impression by his quiet, reasonable manner. Chicago's Mayor Richard Daley praised him as a "fighter for freedom and for peace in the Middle East." Egyptian-American relations had never been so cordial.

The Palestinians, meanwhile, were scoring their own public relations points. On November 25, 1975, backed by the oil-rich Arab nations, they persuaded Third World and Communist delegates in the UN General Assembly to pass a resolution condemning Zionism as "racism," ostensibly because it discriminated against Palestinians. The Israeli ambassador denounced the vote as an attempt to make anti-Semitism respectable.

UN Ambassador Daniel Patrick Moynihan snapped, "The United States rises to declare before the General Assembly of the United Nations and before the world that it does not acknowledge, it will not abide by, it will never acquiesce in this infamous act."

Meanwhile the battle of terror and counterterror raged on. Charging the Fedayeen in Lebanon with organizing new attacks against Israel, the Israelis sent thirty jet fighters over refugee camps in southern Lebanon, strafing men and women at work and children at play. Over 109 people were killed, touching off a storm of international protest.

"I would have to say it was a mistake," admitted General Aharon Yariv, former chief of Israeli military intelligence.

In late December 1975 Palestinian terrorists protested against any Arab cooperation with Israel by seizing the Vienna headquarters of the Organization of Petroleum Exporting Countries (OPEC), killing three people and taking eleven important Arab leaders hostage on a flight to the Middle East before releasing them unharmed.

Arab riots erupted in the West Bank in May 1976. Club-swinging Israeli police charged youthful demonstrators as Israeli troops yanked Arabs by the hair and fired at Arab teenagers. Seen on the world's TV screens, these scenes of brutality shocked Israel's supporters. Even Israel's weekly *Haolam Hazeh* accused the Israeli army and police of "killing innocent people in cold blood."

Syria suffered a black eye in the Arab world when President Hafez Assad sent Syrian troops into Lebanon, ostensibly to restore peace in the Lebanese civil war, but actually to prevent the revolutionary PLO forces there from crushing the Christian troops and setting up a radical regime that would force war with Israel, involving Syria.

For a violence-weary world, the dream of peace in the Middle East was still an endless nightmare.

# 12

# The Helping Hand from Moscow

THE WORSE RELATIONS grew between the Arab world and the United States, Britain, and France, the better they became with the Soviet Union. The Arabs were pleased when the Russians, after first supporting the Israelis, later opposed them. Soviet offers of military and technical help were welcomed by Arab nationalist leaders who came to power eager to make the Arab world strong, modern, and united.

The Soviet system of full employment through socialism greatly impressed Arab college graduates who were unable to find suitable job opportunities in the Middle East.

The Russians, in turn, were eager for influence in the Arab world. The oil-rich Gulf states offered a source of international power, not only through access to this energy storehouse, but also through encouraging the Arabs to cut back supplies of oil to

the West. The more Arab nations that could be persuaded to become Communist, the stronger the Soviet world position would
become. The Russians also hoped to win Arab nuclear bases in
the Middle East to offset those the United States had built in
Europe, Turkey, and the Mediterranean.

During the Cold War, American foreign policy sought to
undermine Soviet influence among the Arabs. During a Middle
East visit for this purpose in May 1953, Secretary of State John
Foster Dulles was annoyed to find the Arabs "more fearful of
Zionism than of the Communists." The United States offered
financial aid and arms only to those conservative Arab countries
it could count on as anti-Soviet.

From 1955 to 1958 the Russians sought to counter American
and British influence by supporting the Syrian and Egyptian
governments, and aiding revolution in Iraq. The Soviet Union
offered its own policies as a model for radical Arab aspirations — independence from the West, and domestic strength
through planned industrialization and social welfare.

Courted by both the Soviet Union and the United States as
leader of the Arab bloc, Nasser vacillated between them, playing off one against the other to get the most aid for Egypt on the
best terms. By 1956 there were over fifteen hundred Soviet
technicians and advisors in Cairo. When Dulles decided to
withdraw his offer of an American loan to build the Aswan High
Dam, the Russians stood behind theirs, and for a while Egypt
slipped into the Soviet orbit.

In July 1957 the anti-American defense minister of Syria,
Khalid Azm, went to Moscow to negotiate an economic agreement. The Russians provided the Syrians with technical aid and
substantial credits for constructing dams and power stations, developing oil and mineral fields, setting up fertilizer factories,
and building a railroad. The treaty, hailed joyfully in Damascus,
convinced Washington that Syria was going Communist.

One week later the Syrian government accused the United States of plotting to overthrow the regime. Three diplomats of the United States embassy were expelled for approaching Syrian officials to enlist them in a coup. The United States responded by expelling the Syrian ambassador. Dulles announced arms shipments to Lebanon, Iraq, and Saudi Arabia to counter a "major build-up of arms in Syria."

The Communists also gained influence in Iraq in 1958 with the overthrow of the monarchy by left-wing Abdul Karim Kassem. Arab leaders grew increasingly uneasy, however, about accepting arms, training, and supervision from the Russians in support of their conflict with Israel. Fearful of becoming Middle East satellites of Moscow, they also worried about the influence of communism among the impoverished masses. These fears drove Syria's Baath party to seek protection in the alliance with Egypt that produced the United Arab Republic.

Relations between Russia and Egypt worsened sharply when Nasser began attacking all Middle East Communists as subversives, warning, "The Arab people who fought for liberation from imperialism will never agree to become satellites."

Soon Kassem, too, turned against the Communists in Iraq, despite large-scale economic and military aid from the Soviet Union. Blocked in Iraq, Syria, and Egypt, Premier Nikita Khrushchev decided that the Russians' best chance of retaining influence in the Middle East was to patch things up with Nasser.

That was why in August 1960 the Soviet Union offered to pay for almost the whole cost of the Aswan Dam. Nasser's anti-Communist rhetoric softened appreciably, and by 1965 he was promised large-scale military aid from Moscow. The following year the Russians also found a new welcome in Syria, where the regime had become publicly committed to supporting the revolutionary warfare strategy of Al Fatah.

While aiding the revolutionary Arab camp, Moscow tried to

prevent guerrilla warfare from escalating into full-scale war with Israel, because that might drag in the United States and result in a nuclear confrontation. When the Six-Day War broke out in 1967, hasty consultations over the "hot line" between the White House and the Kremlin resulted in promises that each power would restrain its Middle East ally. On June 24, to the chagrin of Nasser and other Arab leaders, all Soviet military aid to Egypt was halted.

When Sadat succeeded Nasser, the Russians sped a mission to Cairo with a treaty of friendship, which Sadat signed reluctantly. The Soviet Union encouraged Arab resistance to a peace accord with Israel. As long as turmoil continued in the Middle East, the Arab nations would need Soviet aid, assuring a Russian military presence in that part of the world.

In March 1970 some fifteen thousand Soviet military personnel began manning antiaircraft defenses for the Egyptian armed forces. Worried by the Russian decision to "inject their own combat manpower into the area," Kissinger expressed concern that "the eastern Mediterranean might become a Soviet lake."

But the Russian technicians, who were often high-handed in their dealing with the Egyptians, soon became as unpopular as the British had once been. Anti-Russian sentiment intensified after Sadat, prodded by his army officers, asked for new offensive armaments as sophisticated as those with which the United States was supplying Israel. Moscow rejected the request, fearful Egypt might use them to start a new war.

The Russians by now were moving toward a policy of détente with the United States, and were reluctant to jeopardize its chances by fueling a new Middle East conflict. The Arabs suspected Moscow of preparing to sell out their interests for the sake of a new Soviet-American relationship.

In July 1972 Sadat ordered the immediate withdrawal of some forty thousand Soviet military personnel and their families, putting the Egyptian army in control of Soviet bases and equipment. He also purged Egyptian leftists he accused of plotting to overthrow him. In a radio broadcast Sadat made it clear that Egypt intended to exercise full control of its own affairs. The Russians, deprived overnight of the main base for their Middle East presence, sought to compensate for the setback by stepping up their activities in Syria and Iraq.

The Palestinians, like the Egyptians, also grew disillusioned with the Soviet Union. When Black September and other violent Fedayeen groups began their terrorist crusade in Europe, Moscow called their attacks "ill-advised actions . . . which discredit the resistance movement" and aided "reactionary groupings which seek to play up the disagreements among the Arabs." PLO radicals turned away from Moscow to Peking, which was not slow to offer encouragement. Arab terrorist tactics increasingly took on the aspects of guerrilla warfare as Mao had practiced it against the Chinese Nationalists.

The Russians nevertheless remained the chief supplier of arms for all Arab countries except Jordan, Lebanon, Saudi Arabia, and the Gulf sheikhdoms, which looked to the West for their weapons. Even pro-American Lebanon, late in 1971, decided to buy some Soviet armaments.

When the Yom Kippur War broke out in October 1973, the Russians felt obliged to undertake a massive resupply operation for Egypt and Syria by air and sea, while the United States reequipped Israel. But both superpowers sought to defuse the explosive conflict in a joint communiqué of July 1974:

"Both sides believe that the removal of the danger of war and tension in the Middle East is a task of paramount importance and urgency, and therefore, the only alternative is the achievement, on the basis of UN Security Council Resolution 338, of a just and lasting peace settlement in which should be taken into account the legitimate interests of all peoples in the Middle East, including the Palestinian people, and the right to existence of all states in the area.''

Sadat's foreign minister, Ismail Fahmy, subsequently visited Moscow with a list of economic and military assistance needed by Egypt. When he handed this list to Premier Leonid Brezhnev, the Russian leader presented him with a list of anti-Soviet quotations from the Cairo press, and with statements detailing Egypt's overdue 4.4-billion-dollar debt to the USSR. The conference broke up after only thirty-four chilly minutes.

Sadat indicated that Soviet military aid was now of much lesser importance than Kissinger's diplomatic efforts.

"The Russians can give you arms," he told an aide, "but only the United States can give you a solution."

When Kissinger's initial efforts at shuttle diplomacy failed to bring about an immediate step-by-step Middle East peace settlement, the Russians sought to increase their own influence by engineering a full-scale peace conference at Geneva. Soviet diplomats went to Tel Aviv in April 1975 to urge the Israelis to support it as the only alternative to another Mideast war. Moscow was willing to guarantee Israel's survival as a nation if the Israelis agreed to return to their 1967 borders. The Israelis were not interested.

The Russians invited leaders of Iraq, Syria, and the PLO to Moscow, but these efforts to warm up Arab-Soviet relations failed. Moscow supported Qaddafi's feud with Sadat by selling Libya $800 million worth of Soviet jets, tanks, missiles, and submarines. But Qaddafi, a militant anti-Communist, ignored a Russian request for Libyan air and naval bases.

To add to Soviet chagrin, in August North Yemen requested the withdrawal of Soviet military experts advising its army, and Syria began replacing one hundred Soviet oil experts with Western technologists. Moscow's increasing displeasure with the Arab nations was indicated in September when Sadat was denied an extension on a $200 million arms debt he owed.

The chief mistake made by the Russians in their bid to establish a power base in the Middle East was their belief that the strong Arab hatred of Western imperialism would make the anti-Western banners of Soviet communism welcome. Arab nationalists proved willing enough to play off one side against the other, but refused to mortgage their independence to any outside power. The Communist party, denounced for its subservience to Moscow, was made illegal almost everywhere in the Arab world.

Most Arab leaders grew to recognize that while American aid came with a political price tag, Soviet aid came with a leash and collar.

The incompatibility of Arabs and Russians had even deeper roots. Most Arab leaders and the masses of Arabs were devout Moslems, and as such held the atheism of the Communists in abhorrence. If a few Arab radicals were willing to follow the teachings and inheritors of Marx, Lenin, or Mao, the vast majority of Arabs continued to respond to the age-old cry: *"Laa ilaaha illa llaah!"*

For them there was, indeed, no God but Allah.

# 13

## The Arab Superweapon --Oil

GEOLOGISTS ESTIMATE that more than half the earth's known reserves of oil, the world's chief source of energy, are locked under the sands of the Middle East. Iraq, Libya, and the kingdoms of the Arabian Peninsula are the major oil producers of the Arab world. Egypt, Syria, Lebanon, and Jordan all receive income from the movement of oil through the Suez Canal or overland by pipeline, so that oil is of the greatest importance to most of the Arab nations.

The United States depends upon foreign oil for up to twenty percent of its needs, and some experts think this figure will double before the turn of the century. Europe depends on Middle East oil for two-thirds of its supply, making it far more vulnerable to Arab political and price pressures.

The first important oil strike in the Middle East took place in

1908 in non-Arab Iran, then called Persia. In a deal with the Persian government, the British quickly organized a monopoly, the Anglo-Iranian Oil Company. Just before World War I, geological surveys indicated that vast reserves of oil lay under not only Iran but also under most of the Arab territories adjacent to the Persian Gulf.

Following that war, Britain and France recarved the borders of the Middle East to give Britain control of Iraqi oil, with twenty-five percent of the profits going to France. Washington, warned by a geological survey that America's own oil reserves were precarious, negotiated a deal with the British Foreign Office that gave American oil companies a working partnership in the Iraqi enterprise.

As the liquid "black gold" gushed from the oil wells in Iraq, that country began bursting out of its ancient Turkish stagnation, developed swiftly by oil revenues into a rich and thriving modern nation. In 1928 the international partners in the Iraq Petroleum Company — Exxon, Mobil, Gulf, Anglo-Iranian, Royal Dutch, and Compagnie Française — agreed to protect their monopoly by not developing oil fields independently, thus keeping world oil prices artificially high by avoiding competition among themselves.

The 1928 cartel expanded operations until it controlled virtually every aspect of the production, refining, and marketing of most of the world's oil for the next decade.

By arrangement with the cartel in 1933, American oil interests — Standard Oil of California, Texaco, Exxon, and Mobil — were allowed to exploit the Saudi Arabian oil fields. Organized into the Arabian-American Oil Company (ARAMCO), they were interlocked with the Iraq Petroleum Company, expanding the monopoly. Ibn Saud, not trusting Westerners fully, demanded a down payment for the concession of thirty-five thousand gold sovereigns, which his foreign minister counted at a table, one by one.

American geologists dressed in Arab clothes, grew thick beards, and had the protection of Ibn Saud's soldiers as they spent months and years searching for oil by camel caravan. They quickly learned to respect the hard, simple life of Bedouin tribesmen.

With no refrigeration, canned meats quickly became rank in the desert. As for water, geologist Krug Henry recalled, "If you've tasted water after it's sloshed around for a while in a goatskin bag, hairside-in, you've tasted something. But we *had* to have water, so we just held our noses and swallowed quick."

When the Americans first began the search for oil in Saudi Arabia, the country's income was derived from raising livestock for subsistence, several million date palms, and whatever could be earned from the yearly influx of Mecca-bound pilgrims. There was no skilled bureaucracy to help set up the enormous, complicated structure needed for oil operations.

The cartel distrusted Western-educated Arabs, who might unionize Bedouin workers or agitate to nationalize the oil fields. To educate the workers it needed, the cartel built primary schools that limited education to the eighth grade, and a few secondary schools to train a carefully screened minority for higher positions. ARAMCO also began building ports, highways, airfields, a railroad, hospitals, and utilities, and encouraged Arab entrepreneurs to open small businesses.

When oil began gushing out of the sands of Saudi Arabia, it quickly brought the Saud dynasty more wealth in a single year than all the frankincense and myrrh had ever earned for the peninsula in all its years of habitation.

In 1938 rich oil deposits were also located in Kuwait, near where pearl divers in the Persian Gulf had for centuries brought up globs of pitch that Bedouins boiled and smeared on their camels as a poultice for mange, not recognizing it as oil.

"If we had not had this development of nature, thanks be to God," said Kuwaiti official Rashid Abdulaziz Alrashid, "we probably all would still be pearl divers."

Kuwait was allocated to the British to develop. They sent illiterate young Bedouin tribesmen to an oil training school, where they were drilled in arithmetic even before they learned to read and write. After rigorous schooling, the Kuwaitis were given jobs as riggers, typists, drivers, electricians, bulldozer operators, telephone operators, lathe workers, and laboratory assistants. Few, however, were permitted to rise to managerial positions.

The Arab nations, delighted by their new oil wealth, naturally wanted the Western oil men to keep exploring for new fields. Iraq and Kuwait passed a law requiring them to drill a certain number of exploratory wells a year. But the world depression of the 1930s sent the price of oil plunging, despite the oil cartel. New oil discoveries in Texas and the Mexican Gulf also threatened to glut the market, driving prices down still further.

To suppress oil production, the cartel deceived the Arab nations by a "dry hole strategy," drilling the required number of shallow wells on locations where they knew from geology reports that there was no oil. Arab governments wondered at the oil men's prolonged streak of "bad luck."

When World War II crippled Middle East oil production, ARAMCO found it unprofitable to continue obligatory payments to Saudi Arabia for concession rights. Company executives solved the problem by secretly getting the American government instead to pay King Saud through Lend Lease funds.

Subsequently Saud demanded more money, and ARAMCO worked out another way to pay him without costing the company a cent of profits. The oil lobby won passage of a tax bill by

Congress that allowed ARAMCO to pay increased "taxes" to Saudi Arabia, then deduct them as a "tax credit" from the amount of taxes it owed the United States Treasury. The oil tax dollars of which the Treasury was deprived were made up from the pockets of American taxpayers, who in effect were forced to subsidize King Saud for the benefit of the oil companies.

Following World War II, increased world demands for oil spurred new development, and drill crews worked around the clock in the Arabian Peninsula. In 1946 hard-pressed Arab workmen staged a work stoppage for higher wages and better conditions. The Saudi government passed antistrike laws, with compulsory dismissal, prison sentences, and deportation among the penalties for striking.

The laws did not prevent a strike in 1953, sparked by Nasser's call from Egypt for revolution. Saud declared martial law on the oil fields, arresting one hundred strike leaders. Arab anger was channeled away from ARAMCO and toward the Saudi government, which was receiving and lavishly spending great wealth earned by the sweat of Bedouin labor.

There was trouble with Arab tribesmen in Syria, too, where a trans-Arabian pipeline was being built to carry oil across miles of desert from the wellheads. Hundreds who could not get jobs formed a mob that descended on a pipeline camp demanding food. Denied it, they stormed the mess in a riot that turned into an all-out attack on the oil company outpost, which was looted and burned down.

The cartel not only monopolized oil production, but also owned and controlled the pipelines and tanker fleets necessary to transport oil to world markets. The Big Three of the cartel, Exxon, Anglo-Iranian, and Royal Dutch–Shell, controlled two-thirds of the world's privately owned tankers.

A threat to the Western oil cartel arose in 1951. Becoming prime minister of Iran, Mohammed Mossadegh tore up his country's agreement with the Anglo-Iranian Oil Company as "unholy and unjust," and nationalized Iran's oil industry. Anglo-Iranian withdrew its technicians and key equipment to prevent production. Other cartel members denied the Iranians access to tankers and markets. Mossadegh appealed to Washington for help. The American oil lobby saw a chance to increase the American share of the international cartel.

The CIA, working in secret with the Iranian army, organized "spontaneous" uprisings against Mossadegh, who was overthrown and arrested. In an arrangement with the Shah, Iranian oil was restored to the control of Anglo-Iranian, but now with American oil companies included as partners.

In 1952 the United States Department of Justice filed an antitrust suit against American members of the cartel known as the Seven Sisters — Exxon, Mobil, Socal, Gulf, Texaco, British Petroleum (BP), and Shell (British-Dutch). They were charged with operating like private governments in the Middle East.

"The cartel arrangements are in effect private treaties negotiated by private companies for whom the profit incentive is paramount," the indictment read. "The national security should rest instead upon decisions made by the government with primary concerns for the national interest."

But the powerful oil lobby persuaded President Dwight D. Eisenhower that their cartel was vital to national security. Quashing the indictment, he wrote in a memo, "The enforcement of the antitrust laws of the United States against the Western oil companies operating in the Near East may be deemed secondary to the national interest."

ARAMCO built three American outposts in the desert of Saudi Arabia. The oil cities of Abqaiq, Ras Tanura, and Dhahran were distinguished by green lawns, thick hedges, and air-conditioned homes, schools, hospitals, theaters, clubs, and offices. ARAMCO oil executives enjoyed close personal contacts with King Saud, who declared, "All Americans are welcome to my country. They are like my own people to me."

In 1960 the Seven Sisters, faced with new competition from private oil companies, strengthened their cartel by creating the Organization of Petroleum Exporting Companies (OPEC) to control the world price of oil. Ostensibly, OPEC's members were the Arab oil-producing governments themselves. In reality, OPEC was controlled by the Seven Sisters and a few independents invited to join, rather than fight, the club.

After Israel's victory in the 1967 Six-Day War, the Arab nations imposed an oil embargo against the United States and Israel's other allies in Western Europe, to compel Israel's withdrawal from occupied Arab territories. The boycott failed when Algeria and Tunisia continued selling oil to Europe, and the oil cartel decided to increase production in Venezuela and Africa. The United States was able to get its twenty percent of imported oil without difficulty.

Fearful of losing their oil markets, Saudi Arabia and Kuwait abandoned the embargo by the end of June; other Arab oil countries quickly followed suit. Meeting in Sudan in August, the Arab leaders decided that an oil boycott could succeed as a political weapon only if *all* oil-producing nations, including non-Arab countries, were brought into OPEC, making it a worldwide cartel.

Led by Sheikh Zaki Yamani, Saudi Arabia's minister of oil and mineral wealth, OPEC enlisted Venezuela, Indonesia, Iran, and other non-Arab oil-producing nations as members. Yamani also united the Arab nations behind demands that compelled the oil companies to surrender an increasing share of stock and profits in Arab oil operations. OPEC was now no longer a mere front for manipulations by the Seven Sisters.

In 1968 economists working for Standard Oil of California recommended that the cartel increase oil profits by "strong measures to prevent an oversupply of crude oil, including production cutbacks." They predicted, "All of the major international companies would act concurrently to hold production down rather than see prices drop."

To the embarrassment of the oil lobby, this memo surfaced in a congressional hearing in March 1974, after the United States had suffered a severe oil shortage because of an OPEC boycott. It did little to reassure the American public that the oil companies were trying to increase oil supplies.

Qaddafi alarmed the oil cartel in 1969 by demanding a twenty percent increase in royalties and taxes on Libyan oil production. The cartel resisted until agreement by independent oil companies forced them to go along. Immediately the Persian Gulf nations — Iran, Saudi Arabia, Kuwait, and others — demanded and had to be pacified with equal increases. Libya then won a second raise, which had to be granted the others. In a few years Arab oil revenues soared by three hundred percent.

The cartel was also forced to yield increasing shares in the oil companies, making the Arab nations genuine partners instead of just fronts. The cartel suffered no loss in profits, however, because every rise in oil costs was passed along to consumers, with the oil companies sharing in Arab profits.

The cartel was badly shaken in June 1972 when Iraq passed a law that let the government take over all oil fields, pumping stations, and pipelines owned by the Iraq Petroleum Company. Syria followed suit by nationalizing all the company's property in its territory. And Kuwait arbitrarily cut back oil production so that its reserves would last longer.

"We must plan oil extraction in accordance with our ability to absorb the money we take," declared Sheikh Ramani for the Arab nations in OPEC. "We must use this income to further the fastest economic development of the country."

Two days after Egypt's Yom Kippur attack on Israel in October 1973, Arab members of OPEC voted to use their oil as a weapon in support of the Arab armies. A twenty-five percent cutback was imposed on all Arab oil production, along with a four hundred percent increase in the price of oil to over ten dollars a barrel. An oil embargo was imposed on shipments to the United States, Europe, and Japan until Israel was forced to consent to implementing UN Security Council Resolution 242, calling upon Israel to evacuate its territory taken in the 1967 war.

The oil weapon proved a powerful device this time, creating a critical shortage in a world already running low in energy fuels. Countries competed with each other desperately to secure oil from non-Arab sources. Hardest hit were Japan, England, Italy, and Germany, whose industries ran on Middle East oil. Sky-high prices also doomed the industrial hopes of developing nations in Asia and Africa, and deprived them of oil-based fertilizers needed for agriculture.

The Saudis sought to moderate the boycott in favor of the United States. But when the White House asked Congress to rush military aid to Israel, King Faisal continued to ban Saudi Arabian oil shipments to the Americans.

The United States and the rest of the world were, for the first time, forced to recognize the oil power of the Arabs to dislocate the economies of entire nations overnight. The Arabs were now regarded as a force to reckon with as they had never been since the days of the Islamic Empire. For once Arab leaders did not succumb to their weakness for quarreling among themselves and destroying their unity. They now recognized that as long as they held together, OPEC would be too powerful to be broken by Western opposition, or by Western efforts to bribe members to break away.

In its struggle with Western governments, OPEC had the silent support of its Western business partners, who were acting against the interests of their own nations. As Senator Frank

Church later reported, the major oil companies had no interest in destroying the OPEC cartel which profited them as well as the Arab governments, and which also charged them less for oil than the independent oil companies had to pay.

During the 1973 embargo Arab oil cost ARAMCO only $ .12 a barrel to produce, resulting in corporation profits of $1.23 a barrel. "These were profits *after* the payment of royalties and taxes to the Arabian governments," reported Shirley Ward of the United States General Accounting Office.

At the height of the oil crisis the Saudis insisted that ARAMCO cut off all deliveries to the United States Navy's Sixth Fleet in the Mediterranean. ARAMCO obeyed, forcing the Pentagon to ask British Petroleum to supply the navy's needed oil.

Senator Frank Church's Subcommittee on Multinational Corporations also noted that when King Faisal demanded to know how much ARAMCO oil from Saudi Arabia went to the United States military, so that Faisal could cut back production by that amount, ARAMCO provided this secret military information.

"In time of war that's called treason," said a member of the Church subcommittee. Ironically, Washington had given huge tax benefits, plus immunity from antitrust laws, to the big American oil companies, on the ground that supporting their activities in the Middle East was essential to America's national defense.

Americans were shocked by the impact the OPEC boycott and higher oil prices had on their lives. It became a daily struggle for many to find enough gas to drive cars to work. Some states rationed purchases to every other day. Highway speed limits were sharply reduced to conserve gas. Prices at the gas pump soared, along with the cost of home heating oil. Families struggling to make ends meet were forced to turn down home thermostats and wear sweaters.

Angry Americans demanded to know why the government had not foreseen the vulnerability of the United States to an Arab boycott, and developed enough independent oil sources to prevent such energy "blackmail." Washington sought to divert public wrath to the Arabs, blaming them for the crisis.

But two out of three barrels of oil used in the United States were produced domestically. The oil companies raised the price of domestic oil along with imported oil, increasing their profits in 1973 to eight billion dollars. They denied rumors that they were deliberately creating an artificial shortage in order to have an excuse to profiteer.

"The American people have a right to know the truth," challenged Senator Henry Jackson. "We cannot expect people to stand in line for gasoline when there are allegations that storage tanks are full and there are fully loaded tankers lying off many ports."

After the Arab-Israeli cease-fire took effect early in March 1974, seven of the nine Arab OPEC nations met in Vienna and voted to lift the oil embargo. But they rejected appeals from consumer nations to roll back prices, which remained at a world-record high. In a speech at the UN in April, Dr. Saadoun Hammadi, Iraq's minister of oil and minerals, defended the Arab countries against charges of profiteering and of causing worldwide inflation.

The Arab nations had been forced to raise oil prices, Hammadi insisted, to pay the higher prices the Western countries were charging for manufactured products. Moreover, all the Arabs had to offer the world was oil, a treasure that was being depleted every year. If they did not make the most of it while they still had it, the Arab nations would be left far behind in the struggle for economic development.

"Who would have supposed that the Arab countries could have thrown the United States into such a tailspin?" asked

Senator Ernest Hollings in January 1975. "In fact, they have not done it alone. The Arabs could never have succeeded without substantial help from . . . the multinational major oil companies, with Secretary of the Interior Rogers C. B. Morton and Treasury Secretary William E. Simon following the time-honored tradition of giving the oil companies everything they want, and making the American people pay through the nose."

He added, "It's easy to point the finger at the OPEC nations as a scapegoat for our own domestic failures. But the Arabs are only using their economic wealth in a logical and powerful manner. It's the one weapon they have, and the multinational corporations which deal directly with them respect it. By contrast, our own so-called energy leaders have been pushovers for Big Oil."

Washington, however, continued to react with shock and outrage at the Arab use of the oil weapon. On January 6, 1974, Secretary of Defense James Schlesinger warned that the United States might consider using force if the Arabs again sought to shut off Western oil "to cripple the larger mass of the industrialized world." Kissinger, declaring that he was reflecting the views of President Ford, added, "I'm not saying there's no circumstance where we would not use force," because "it is self-evident that the United States cannot permit itself to be strangled."

Outraged, Kuwait's Foreign Minister Sheikh Sabah declared that he would blow up Kuwait's oil installations if the Americans invaded his country. Egyptian editor Mohammed Hassanein Heikal predicted that if the United States landed forces in the Middle East, American protest would shake Washington.

"It would backfire," he warned, "and make the Bay of Pigs and Vietnam seem like picnics."

Arab spokesmen spread the word that the vast oil fields of the Persian Gulf region had been mined to self-destruct. American intervention would allegedly turn a twenty-billion-dollar net-work of refineries, pipelines, storage tanks, pumps, and super-tanker docks into instant worthless junk.

Throughout 1974 rumors of another Arab oil boycott inspired counterrumors of American military reprisals. In March 1975 United States Ambassador to Saudi Arabia James Akins de-clared, "The threats to occupy the oil fields and the press cam-paign which accompanied them were caused by persons with sick minds who do not know what they say." He castigated all such threats of invasion of the Middle East as criminal in nature.

That did not prevent the Pentagon, in the fall of 1975, from sending United States special forces to West Germany to par-ticipate in maneuvers involving the seizure of oil fields.

In an effort to force OPEC oil prices down, Kissinger at-tempted to organize the oil-consuming nations into a unified bloc. He failed because many Western countries feared being punished by an Arab oil boycott. In October 1975 OPEC met and once more raised oil prices an additional ten percent.

The world's oil-producing and oil-consuming nations finally met in a Paris conference in December, and agreed to set up committees to explore ways of tying the price of oil needed by the West to the prices of food and manufactures needed by the East. An East-West accord was hoped for by 1977–78.

Meanwhile, high prices for oil were flooding the OPEC na-tions with wealth that accumulated faster than it could be in-vested. The London *Economist* estimated that they were piling up reserves at the rate of $115,000 every second — fast enough to buy the Bank of America in six days, and every major com-pany in the world in less than sixteen years.

# 14

# Black Gold and the Arab People

UNFORTUNATELY FOR the vast majority of Arabs, oil riches are thickest where the population is thinnest. The chief beneficiaries are 100,000 people in Qatar, 200,000 in Bahrain, 230,000 in the United Arab Emirates, 600,000 in Oman, 1,000,000 in Kuwait, 2,000,000 in Libya, and 5,300,000 in Saudi Arabia. But all these together add up to less than a fourth of the impoverished population of Egypt alone.

Oil income puts about fifty billion dollars a year into the treasuries of the luckier Arab nations. Since these "petro-dollars" are far more than can be absorbed all at once in de-veloping the recipient countries, the Arabs have sought to invest the surplus in Western economies.

In 1975 rumors spread that they were planning to buy up General Motors. Said one rich Arab potentate, "Yes, we would buy General Motors, but the Zionists are so powerful in America that they would force the government to nationalize it."

That apprehension, however, did not prevent Saudi Arabia from becoming part owner of Delta Airlines. Arab faith in the American economy, moreover, was strong enough to let the Saudis purchase $200 million worth of United States government bonds.

Kuwaitis invested in a ten-million-dollar hotel-office complex in Atlanta, purchased twenty-six million dollars' worth of Boston buildings, and bought Kiawah Island off South Carolina for seventeen million dollars, planning to develop it as a resort community. When South Carolinians raised a storm of protest over Arab ownership of a community in their midst, Arab oil man Reda Thabet charged, "It is racism." He pointed out that foreign investors who were European met no such American opposition.

Lebanese Roger Tamraz, a graduate of Harvard Business School, attempted to buy a hundred-million-dollar interest in Lockheed Aircraft for Arab clients. He was stopped by Washington on grounds that the second largest American defense contractor could not be allowed to pass into Arab hands.

Most Arabs were convinced that the reason the American press had been unsympathetic toward their wars with Israel was that it was Zionist-owned. One Saudi Arabian sheikh asked London painter Nicholas Egon plaintively, "Do you think it would help if we bought the *New York Times?*"

Ghaith Pharaon, son of one of King Khalid's chief advisors, bought control of Detroit's one-billion-dollar Bank of the Commonwealth, which had fifty-seven branches throughout Michigan. The purchase fueled such resentment in the financial community that two subsequent Arab attempts to buy United States banks were thwarted.

"Our nation has become an international supermarket with our businesses on sale at bargain-basement prices," protested Representative Joseph Gaydos. Two dozen bills to curb Arab investment in the United States were introduced in Congress, but failed. The State Department then pressed for a bill to limit the foreign control of any American business to ten percent.

Arab businessmen viewed these moves as reflecting a hypocritical double standard for a country that had never hesitated to buy controlling interests in Arab or other foreign enterprises. "America built its own prosperity by investing abroad," pointed out industrialist Adnan Khashoggi of Saudi Arabia. "Now they are reluctant to export their system."

One Arab editor, Mohammed Hassanein Heikal, indicated that Arab wealth may have purchased influence in the White House in 1972–73. In his newspaper, the Cairo *Al Ahram,* he revealed that ex-President Richard Nixon had campaigned for reelection with twelve million dollars in funds secretly contributed by Arab donors.

Most Arabs who came to the United States to invest oil wealth sought to do so inconspicuously, shunning publicity in the belief that deals were best made quietly. When a reporter tried to see one Arab tycoon, he was told on the phone, "We are a very simple people. We want few things. We are not interested in kings, or presidents, or publicity. We want no more friends, no more enemies. We came from the desert, we go back to the desert. We want unmarked graves. Good-bye."

American executives who flew to Saudi Arabia seeking business deals found negotiations frustrating. The phone service was so inadequate that it often took up to three days for overseas calls back to their offices. Some American executives were forced to fly to Athens to find a working phone.

Ansbert G. Skina, president of the United States–Arab Chamber of Commerce, cautioned American executives going to the Middle East to do business for the first time: "It takes much time to understand the many small and subtle ways in which differences of reaction, behavior and type of thought affect everyday business life. In the first place, you must face the fact that you will always be an outsider. . . . Your cue is to be at your best: i.e., no familiarity or questionable jokes, no loud or boastful displays, no first names or 'instant friendship.' What is required is reasonable behavior and courtesy. . . . It will not hurry anything to push. It is better to sip tea, remain casual, patient, but study your associate carefully while he studies you."

Editor Mohammed Hassanein Heikal offered further insight into the psychology of newly rich Arabs: "The oil producers are like the man who has made a great fortune out of the blue. He feels everyone wants to grab it away from him. The right approach for the Western countries is the French one—reassure the Arabs and don't rattle them."

He told of visiting a Geneva mansion bought by a wealthy Arab who kept touching everything as if unable to believe it was all his. The tycoon said, "You know, I feel that I'm on a movie set and that as soon as the filming is over a crew is going to come in and take it all away." Heikal observed, "That reflects an Arab syndrome today—too good to be true. America should pay more heed to the psychological factor."

Like all newly rich, the Arabs delight in the luxuries their money can buy. Some collect Rolls-Royces, Mercedes-Benzes and Aston-Martins. In London they shed their Arab robes for Savile Row suits, and ignore mint tea for dry martinis in $120-a-night-and-up suites of the new lavish Wellington Hotel. Educated in Western universities, many now feel more at home in London, New York, and Paris than in Cairo, Damascus, Beirut, or Riyadh.

One Persian Gulf billionaire bought an eighteenth-century British castle featured in the film *Casino Royale* for over one million dollars. Sheikh Aharif Al-Hamdan of Saudi Arabia, negotiating in Texas to buy the Alamo as a birthday present for his son, was chagrined to find that it was not for sale.

The Sultan of Oman bought $44,000 worth of perfume from Harrods of London for his wives. When the salesgirl warned of the risk of evaporation, he replied with a shrug, "That's all right. It's just for their baths."

One sheikh walked into New York's Saks Fifth Avenue, liked a towel he saw, and ordered $3,000 worth. Another picked up jewelry souvenirs in Tiffany's for his family in Kuwait, and peeled off $70,000 in bills for the stunned cashier. Three Arab princes were alleged to have gambled away a million dollars in cash in just three days at Las Vegas.

But not all Arab wealth was spent abroad in self-indulgence or buying up foreign properties. In Kuwait and Saudi Arabia particularly, the people benefited from elaborate programs of modernization and social benefits.

Under Emir Sabah Al-Salim, Kuwait was transformed from a dusty desert outpost of merchants, sailors, and divers into one of the most modern countries in the world. Smaller than Maryland, it has become a model Arab welfare state, which a national assembly helps the emir to plan.

Kuwait City, once a mud-walled capital, now blazes with light along its wide boulevards and highways. Glass and concrete office buildings, marble banks, theaters, mosques, and public gardens have sprung up everywhere. Not camels but cars race in all directions — one per family, plus eight thousand taxis.

At the ends of the highways, new suburbs rise. Telephone service is free. So are schools, hospitals, and dental clinics. No Kuwaiti lacks a home or job. Any family earning under the minimum considered necessary for a decent standard of living is paid an assistance grant of up to $220 a month, depending on family size. No one pays an income tax.

Most new homes are air-conditioned against Kuwait's fiercely hot weather. Almost a million trees and shrubs have been planted around the capital's sixteen suburbs, turning the desert green and providing a screen against sandstorms. Most Kuwaiti homes enjoy TV, which is watched while sipping mint tea, sitting on the floor.

Many former divers now work on oil rigs, often making as much money in a month as they once made in a year. The opportunities in Kuwait have attracted many Arabs from other lands, as well as Iranians, Indians, and Pakistanis, who fall into the lowest income groups. A $2.25 hourly minimum wage, which may net foreign laborers only squalid shacks on the edge of town, is nevertheless far more than they could earn at home.

Perhaps more than in any other Arab country, the oil revenues won by the emir of Kuwait trickle down to benefit his subjects. Land for new roads, housing developments, office buildings, schools, and government ministries was bought at high prices from its owners, spreading the wealth. Almost three billion dollars was distributed in this manner to small as well as large landowners. One Kuwaiti who had bought his house and land for a modest $5,000 sold it to the government for $105,000.

From dozens of new Kuwaiti mosques the muezzin's call to prayer echoes out across the desert less melodiously than of old, but more powerfully because it is now an electronic recording. All non-Arab faiths are protected in the free exercise of religion, and have their own places of worship. The emir even donated land to help build a Catholic church.

Perhaps no Kuwaiti opportunity is more appreciated than free tuition, from kindergarten to college, in beautiful, modern, and excellently taught schools and the University of Kuwait. School attendance is compulsory for both boys and girls up to age sixteen. In just thirty years oil revenues raised the educational budget in tiny Kuwait from $90,000 annually to today's impressive $95 million a year.

Youth has many practical inducements to excel in studies and enter business. Qualified students are trained free at the Technical College. Graduates are given a handsome bonus to enter government service, and twice that sum if they open their own business.

Although women's liberation is progressing in Kuwait, women do not yet have the vote. A few, however, have been accepted as doctors and in other professions.

Looking ahead to the time when the oil runs out, Kuwait is seeking to diversify its economy, experimenting particularly with hydroponics, or soilless farming, to increase its own food supplies. Spinach, tomatoes, carrots, beets, and cucumbers have been grown in the desert. Fresh water is plentiful in Kuwait, thanks to the erection of the biggest plant in the world for distilling seawater.

The sheikhs of Kuwait tend to feel embarrassed by the world notoriety brought by their oil wealth. "I want the whole world to stop taking so much notice of us here in Kuwait," complained Sheikh Jabir al Ahmad, "and let us live our lives in our own way."

"What we wish to preserve is first our religion," said Sheikh Rashid Abdulaziz Alrashid. "Then our hospitality. Then our family relationships — the feeling of loving and of trying to help and shelter each other. Then, the simplicity of simple men and the respect of the younger for the older. Finally, our individualism — which is both our strength and our weakness — the spirit of independence that encourages even the humblest man to approach the head of state and complain of an injustice. We hope all these will remain."

In Saudi Arabia, part of the oil wealth provides subsidies to some three hundred princes, who lavish vast expenditures on palaces, fleets of limousines, and royal activities. But beneficial uses to which the huge Saudi fortune has been put also include a thirty-million-dollar railroad, two harbors, a radio station, new highways, electric power for four cities, a national airline, water and sewage projects, and the reopening of King Solomon's gold mines near Medina. These enterprises have attracted skilled help from neighboring countries.

Traditional tribal life is giving way to rapid urbanization in the deserts where hardy Bedouin once roamed amid caravans of pilgrims and traders. Workers wishing to settle in their own homes are given twenty-year loans at no interest.

ARAMCO, which has headquarters at Dharan, has been responsible for much of the transformation, building ports, highways, airfields, public utilities, schools, and hospitals. The oil monopoly has also sponsored home ownership, on-the-job training, and aid programs for farmers and small businessmen.

Upper-class Saudis consider air conditioning a necessity in heat that runs as high as 113° by day, 90° by night. But blowing sands are a perpetual problem, clogging up air-conditioner filters. Some modern hotels use triple filters. In summer many Saudi families without air conditioners take to their roofs with rugs for a night's sleep.

In an effort to revive Arabic scholarship, a crash program against illiteracy has tripled the number of Saudi primary and secondary schools. New schools open at the rate of one a day. All education is free, and several thousand Saudi students continue their education at American, European, and Middle East universities, particularly those studying to be engineers.

Girls, who only a dozen years ago received no education at all, now make up a third of students. They are educated separately from boys, however, in the Saudi sexual apartheid that prevents women from working in the same offices as men, and even from driving cars. Nevertheless, in March 1975, a new girls' college in Riyadh graduated the first batch of Saudi women with B.A. degrees, all in the field of education.

Health standards in Saudi Arabia have improved dramatically with the building of clinics, dispensaries, and hospitals around the country. Free medical care and hospitalization is available to all Saudi citizens.

In spite of these advances, Saudi Arabia still remains basically an impoverished, backward, feudal, benevolent despotism. Shantytowns of the poor still surround some of the major cities. Roads, ports, and airports are still so underdeveloped that important supplies are delayed by an archaic hand-labor system of moving shipments.

The Saudis are rushing a seventy-billion-dollar development plan designed to modernize the nation, and industrialize it so that it is less dependent on oil revenues. They even plan to develop solar energy, to preserve their oil for the manufacture of food and fertilizers.

"We have five to eight years to . . . diversify our economy before the world lessens its dependence on us," explained Saudi Planning Minister Isham Nazer in 1975. "There isn't a moment to be lost."

The new Saudi plans also include providing a comfortable home with running water and electricity for everyone in the kingdom. Before his death in 1975 King Faisal declared, "The aim of this government is to do its best for the benefit of the people. . . . We are still in the study, planning and initiation stage. We are still newcomers to the world of efficient administration and scientific development."

Saudi priorities were described by King Khalid as he came to the throne: "Our first duty is to the inhabitants of our kingdom. Then we will take care of the Arab or Moslem countries which are our long-standing neighbors and friends. Then we will help the developing countries without distinction. They deserve our aid more than the rich countries."

Arab leaders of the OPEC cartel were sensitive to the criticism of the developing countries that huge oil price increases had crippled living standards in the Third World.

The wealth of the little Persian Gulf sheikhdom of Qatar is even greater proportionately than that of either Saudi Arabia or Kuwait. The gross national product works out to an average of $21,000 for every man, woman, and child.

Plots of land are given free to Qatar families who want to build their own homes. The one original town, an old fishing village called Doha, has been transformed into an electrified desert city with a showplace twenty-million-dollar hospital, an expert staff and superb equipment. A mass X-ray program has wiped out Qatar's old scourge of TB. But doctors still have problems with Bedouin women who refuse to remove their veils or bare their arms for a hypodermic needle.

Iraq has committed ten billion dollars for a crash agricultural program to increase arable land, water storage, and food production. When a beautiful new public square and ornamental garden were opened in Baghdad not long ago, one Bedouin shepherd drove his flock through the streets to the square, where he put his flock to graze on the new grass. Police drove him off as he protested, "But what else is grass for?"

The Arab "have-not" nations — Egypt, Syria, Lebanon, and Jordan — have proposed schemes for sharing the wealth of their oil-rich brother Arabs. The prosperous Arab nations ignore these proposals, but the Islamic code of generosity has led them to contribute millions toward rebuilding the damaged areas of Egypt and Jordan, and building a rail line in the Sudan, power plants in Tunisia, and an oil pipeline in Algeria.

A major problem for the poorest Arab nations is the population explosion. In Egypt alone there are twice as many people today as there were at the end of World War II. Four times as many Egyptian farmers are trying to live on as small an amount of arable land as in jam-packed Holland.

The swiftly increasing numbers in the Arab countries will need huge new investments of capital and skilled labor to feed, clothe, house, and educate them, and to provide medical care, consumer goods, electricity, running water, roads, and jobs.

Today's Arab masses are less resigned to any fate that "Allah wills," or to living on the edge of starvation through the charity of prosperous Arabs. Radio and TV have informed them of the good life lived by more fortunate Arabs in the oil-rich lands. And does not the Koran teach that no man should raise himself higher than another?

Revolutionary sentiment in the poorer Arab lands makes the wealthy kings of the Middle East nervous. They spend billions of their oil revenues to purchase huge armaments, and strengthen their armies, perhaps to protect themselves less against Israel than against their resentful brethren.

With Hussein, they have not forgotten Nasser's unthinking exclamation: "Wonderful — another Arab king overthrown!"

# 15

# The World Looks at the Arabs

IN 1975, recognizing that they had failed to plead their cause convincingly before the bar of world opinion, Arab leaders began to correct this error with considerable success. Once-solid American support for Israel softened to a more evenhanded attitude toward both sides, and UN sentiment began to swing sharply in favor of the Arab position.

"The main battlefield is the theater of opinion in the United States," acknowledged Israeli General Chaim Herzog in April. The Arab League sent Lebanese journalist Clovis Maksoud on an American lecture tour. "I don't think we can win the hearts of the Americans," he said, "but certainly their minds are open to reason."

Former Israeli Ambassador to the United States Abraham Harman observed, "The Arabs have gotten much cleverer since they dropped the slogan of throwing the Jews into the sea."

A Harris poll in April 1975 revealed that fifty-two percent of Americans still sympathized with Israel, and only seven percent with the Arabs. Political realities kept both major American parties committed to the support of Israel, with politicians of all faiths attending pro-Israeli rallies and dinners.

At a University of Southern California conference, Professor William Quandt, a Middle East specialist, noted that the Jewish vote — over six million — was large enough to determine tight elections, and therefore had to be considered in shaping American foreign policy in the Middle East.

On the other hand, at the end of 1975, when NBC took a poll to determine which countries Americans were willing to go to the defense of if attacked, only twenty-five percent of those questioned said that they were willing to fight for Israel.

The Orthodox branch of Jewry tends to be rigidly against any accommodation with the Arabs. In the United States, Rabbi Fabian Schonfeld, president of the Rabbinical Council of America, charged in April 1975 that Arab students in American universities were conducting "an insidious propaganda campaign" against both Israel and American Jewry. He called upon the State Department to investigate the possibility that many Arab students were acting as agents of their governments.

Moderate American Jewish elements like the Union of American Hebrew Congregations support Israel, but nevertheless make an effort to understand and seek accommodation with the Arabs.

Speaking for UAHC educators, Dr. Dorothy G. Axelroth and Rabbi Leonard A. Schoolman observed, "One can sympathize with the masses of Arab people who suffer poor health, poverty and inadequate education and whose lives and thinking are dominated by irresponsible leaders. Jews committed to the cause of Israel cannot be objective in any study of the Arabs.

However, contempt and hatred of the Arabs can only be a stumbling block in the way of peace and mutual cooperation."

Although the vast majority of American Jews support Israel, non-Zionists and some intellectuals have tended to sympathize more with the plight of the Palestinians. "I don't understand," said one Jewish university student, "how refugees who had suffered so terribly at the hands of the Nazis could themselves make suffering refugees out of the Palestinians."

"The Zionist influence," noted Crown Prince Fahed Ibn Abdul Aziz, Saudi Arabian minister of the interior, "is being faced for the first time with a clear United States resistance, accompanied by a tendency to contact the Arabs and understand their viewpoints. We should encourage this tendency and make it easier for the Americans to understand the facts."

Some prominent Americans began listening to both sides and speaking out. Senator George McGovern, formerly a staunch Israeli supporter, met both the PLO's Arafat and Israeli Prime Minister Rabin in April 1975. "Israel made a strong case," he said afterward, "but I would prefer more flexibility."

So would many Palestinian intellectuals.

"After two decades of warfare," observed Palestinian Henry Cattan, a former UN negotiator, "reasonable men can sit down and work out some form of government that would ensure full rights to all concerned. . . . The details are secondary. It is the will to coexist that is all-important."

"We were evicted," said Palestinian Taher Kanaan, a UN economist. "But we don't want to evict the Jews. In fact, we're not even against new Jews coming into a Palestinian state, subject to immigration laws we can jointly work out."

Egyptian moderates believe that the Israelis are being shortsighted in refusing to allow a Palestinian state to be set up in the occupied West Bank of Jordan. In December 1975 Rabin said flatly, "There will never be room for a third state between

Israel and Jordan. Therefore, I don't see any room for political negotiations with Palestinians."

"The Israelis face a resistance movement on the West Bank that is bound to grow if the occupation continues," warned Dr. Gamel el Oteifi, vice-president of the Egyptian Parliament. "Wouldn't the Israelis rather have a responsible state there that would be recognized by the international community?"

Muhammad Sid Ahmad, political commentator for the newspaper *Al Ahram,* viewed that solution as the best chance to end Palestinian terrorism in the Middle East. "Once they have obtained their own national home . . . violence will die of its own accord," he predicted. "Israel must take a calculated risk, a gamble for peace."

But the Israeli military is reluctant to give up territory won by force of arms. General Ariel Sharon, who masterminded the Israeli thrust across the Suez in 1973, was concerned about the Jewish immigration expected to increase Israel's population to ten million by 1985. To protect them, he insisted, Israel would need the West Bank, the Golan Heights, and the Sinai.

"It is not a question of religion, history, or emotion," he declared. "It is a question of security."

Kissinger urged Americans to make allowances for Israeli apprehension. "People who have lived for twenty-five years," he said, "with the threat of extinction, whose neighbors for its entire history have not recognized its existence, needless to say live with a premonition of catastrophe that is not true of almost any other state. . . . We, as Americans, have to understand it."

In the arena of world opinion, the Russians and the Chinese took opposite sides. Russia's Lev Tokunov, editor of *Izvestia* and a Supreme Soviet deputy, declared, "Almost all the Palestinian organizations have taken a more realistic stand. Many of them believe that if Israel cleared the Western bank of the Jordan and the Gaza Strip, a Palestinian state could be established on the liberated territories."

Communist China believed that Israel's refusal to heed Palestinian demands should be supported. "Israel, which came into existence after being wiped off the earth for over a thousand years, is a *fait accompli*," said Foreign Minister Chiao Kuanhua. "We cannot put the displaced Palestinians back and create an Israeli refugee problem."

Belgian Viscount Etienne Davignon, foreign policy coordinator for the Common Market, expressed the prevailing European view: "Since the 1967 war the majority of people in government came to the conclusion that the Israeli position was excessive, and this is why European opinion shifted from normal sympathy for Israel's extraordinary achievements in making deserts bloom toward distaste for what seemed to be the arrogance of power."

In December 1975 Israeli Labor party members began to respond to changing world opinion by complaining that Rabin was driving Israel into diplomatic isolation by his refusal to deal with the Palestinians.

Blame for the conflict, charged Arafat, lay with the Zionist politicians, not with the Jewish people. He distinguished between the Jews, whom he welcomed as fellow citizens of a new state of Palestine, and the Zionists, whom he did not.

Pressing this distinction at the UN, the Palestinians won a resolution in November 1975 condemning Zionism as "a form of racism and racial discrimination." Israeli Ambassador Chaim Herzog tore up a copy of the resolution, bitterly denouncing it as the anti-Semitic work of "a coalition of despotisms and racists." The resolution was widely repudiated in the West, particularly by the United States.

In the hope of improving understanding between Arabs and Jews, the Foundation for Arab-Israeli Reconciliation in Washington has been bringing together Israeli and Palestinian scholars to discuss and resolve their differences. Continuing contacts between Jews and Arabs at the university level have also been going on in Israel.

Total reconciliation will not come easily; there is bitterness on both sides, neither of which has forgotten or forgiven the other's acts of terrorism.

"We have to recognize that there are no angels in this tragedy," urged Joseph Ben-Dak of Israel's Institute for the Study of International Affairs. "Both sides have sinned against each other. We must now bury the hatchet."

Palestinian Professor Muhammad Rajab, who had close ties with the PLO, predicted that Arabs and Israelis would become warm friends and allies after they began to discuss instead of argue. "Once we get to know each other better," he said, "it is quite amazing to see how many things we have in common."

"Healthy respect for the Arab as a human by the Israelis," suggested a noted Arabist, Professor Charles F. Pfeiffer of Central Michigan University, "will do more than anything else to heal wounds and make cooperation possible."

Many Israelis are already speaking out openly in favor of recognizing the Palestinians and their right to a government of their own. Professor Emanuel Sivan, chairman of the Hebrew University history department, declared, "We do not refuse a Palestinian state on our borders. There is a Palestinian reality that has finally dawned on Rabin."

Joseph Sarid, youngest Labor party member of Israel's Knesset, has also urged his government to make peace with Syria by pledging to remove Israeli armed forces from the Golan Heights within five years. "We could prove to the Syrians our serious intent about the ultimate goal," he said, "by removing two or three civilian settlements there to begin with."

Many university students support the views of Dr. Yehoshofat Harkaby, a leading Israeli scholar and Arabist, who wrote, "To understand the Arab position the Israeli must imagine what he himself would have done if he were an Arab. . . . He must try to estimate in his heart the deep feeling provoked by what the Arabs are convinced was a great outrage. Let him imagine in his heart that he is a Palestinian refugee, uprooted from his environment, where he and his forefathers grew up. . . . Let him try to measure the force of the blow delivered to Arab nationalism (and self-esteem) by Israel's establishment and consolidation."

The Israelis were made aware of growing Arab impatience with their continued occupation of the West Bank in March 1976, when angry Arabs demonstrated and rioted in five West Bank towns, demanding self-government. Their dissatisfaction spread to Arabs within Israel itself, who began protesting their treatment as "second-class citizens."

What are the chances for a final peace settlement?

Some noted Americans were pessimistic that the interim peace agreement worked out by Kissinger between Egypt and Israel would bring genuine peace to the Middle East.

"Can anyone seriously believe," asked former Under Secretary of State George Ball, "that the three million to five million Palestinians scattered throughout the Middle East will let the Arab states do nothing, while Israel continues to occupy the West Bank and the Gaza Strip and progressively incorporates them within her own political and economic system? Or that Syria will sit by placidly while Israel builds more settlements on the Golan Heights? Or that Islam will leave Jerusalem in Israeli hands without a struggle?"

Senator Mike Mansfield was skeptical about the provision of the Sinai agreement requiring two hundred American technicians to man radar units in the UN buffer zone between the Israeli and Egyptian armies. "One Vietnam is too many," he fretted.

Despite stubborn opposition by the leadership on both sides, many Israelis and Palestinians are coming to the conclusion that the most practical solution to the conflict between them is the one Dag Hammarskjold first advocated in 1960 as secretary-general of the UN. This called for an Arab state of Palestine occupying the West Bank, closely tied to Israel in an economic federation.

Israeli Foreign Minister Allon was reported to favor a political and economic federation of Israel, Jordan, and a West Bank Palestinian state. Professor George Assousa of the Foundation for Arab-Israeli Reconciliation declared that the PLO, despite its public stance, was moving toward an acceptance of this solution.

Egyptian editor Butros Ghali believed that the Arab world would accept Israel as a bona fide member of the Middle East if the Israelis joined an Arab version of the Common Market, cutting its ties with Washington. "Israel must decolonize," he declared, "and we must accept it in our midst as a member in good standing of our Middle Eastern community."

"That's an excellent idea that we must grab and run with," agreed Israeli TV commentator Eli Eyal.

"Not only would we be willing but enthusiastic," said Labor party member Joseph Sarid. "Otherwise, peaceful coexistence would be meaningless. Most of us would rather join the area than live as a beleaguered state."

A Middle East Common Market could strengthen both Israel and the Arab nations, providing an enlarged home market for their products. Pooled resources of oil, agriculture, advanced technology, and trained scientists could prosper the whole region. The have-not Arab nations would be helped as a matter of partnership, and as an investment in the stability and development of the Middle East, not as an act of charity.

Sid Ahmad recommended the creation of industrial developments all along the Arab-Israeli borders as part of a Common Market operation, providing peace insurance because no country would want to risk destruction of its valuable industries.

Jerusalem, suggested the Foundation for Arab-Israeli Reconciliation, should become the capital for both Israel and a new state of Palestine, jointly administered with a religious council in charge of the holy places.

The chief obstacles in the way of such Middle East settlements were the unbudging position of leaders on both sides. They feared that willingness to compromise would lay them open to charges of "sellout" from political rivals.

Yet as long as neither side moved toward compromise, the grim prospect could only be for more and bloodier wars. Month by month the weight of armament grew heavier in the Middle East. According to the International Institute for Strategic Studies in London, in July 1975 Israel led the world in per-capita spending on defense, although Egypt spent more of its budget on the military.

In September 1975 the *Congressional Quarterly* reported that American weapons sales were soaring above eight billion dollars a year, over half to the Middle East. American liberals charged Washington with hypocrisy in claiming to work for a Mideast peace settlement. The administration position was that if the United States did not sell these arms, other nations would; also that American peace proposals would be more effective if Middle East nations were dependent upon American, rather than Soviet, spare parts for maintaining armaments.

Accordingly, in March 1976 President Gerald Ford announced the sale of American military transport planes to Egypt, which was feuding with the Soviet Union. "We have to deal with realities," he explained.

The Arab world showed a decided preference for all American-made products. The only large gain in recent American exports was made to Arab markets, in payment for oil imports. Huge increases in sales to the Arab nations were recorded for air-conditioning equipment, iron pipe, farm tractors, office machinery, machine tools, and autos. The popularity of American products was so great in the Middle East that one Lebanese merchant quickly sold out a cargo of slow-moving bananas by deleting the "Central" from "Product of Central America."

Perhaps no force for change has been more potent in the Middle East than the movies, which have shown all classes of Arabs how Western nations live. Egyptian films, portraying the modern style of Arab city life, have also spread dissatisfaction with the ancient, dull wretchedness of village life. Peasant and townsman are equally ardent moviegoers.

Another factor for change has been the rising rate of literacy, which has resulted in greater reading of newspapers and magazines. Village radio has also brought a new awareness of the outside world. Group watching of TV has had an even more direct and dramatic impact. Arab consciousness has been changed and raised by the imprinting of Western images.

The new Arab awakening has led to social change throughout the Middle East. Many peasants have left the land to seek work in city factories and oil complexes. Farmers have been experimenting with Western methods and tools to improve agriculture. Religious authority has declined with the advance of modernization, along with parental authority and male domination. The once-passive Arab masses have demanded social advances which have led some governments toward socialism.

The feminist movement has made gains, with educated

women discarding traditional Arab garb for trim dresses and high-heeled shoes. Princess Ayesha, sister of Morocco's King Hassan, became a leading advocate of freedom for Arab women. In Egypt three thousand married women studied at Cairo University.

"The old tradition of marrying at sixteen and having babies right away is going," declared Mrs. Amina el Said, editor of the Egyptian woman's magazine *Hawaa*. "There was an old saying about the Egyptian woman: She makes two outings in her lifetime — the first time from her parents' home to the home of her husband, and the second from her husband's home to the grave. Now the most respected women in Cairo are those who are educated and working."

The Arabs desperately need swift modernization and industrialization because of their exploding populations, for whom there are not enough farmland or city jobs.

"The only thing that grows in Egypt and stays in the country," a Cairo professor told journalist John Gunther wryly, "is the population. We are a nation smothered by ourselves." In Egypt a million new babies add to the problem every year, despite four thousand government-sponsored family planning clinics in both rural and urban areas.

Unless they are provided for, the masses of Arab poor, angry and frustrated today, might be driven to desperate violence tomorrow. "Within a decade," said former Pakistani President Ayub Khan in 1969, "human beings will eat human beings in Pakistan." Peace is essential if Egypt is to attract the foreign loans and investments it needs to expand its economy. Osman Ahmed Osman, Egypt's minister of reconstruction, hopefully plans to be able to increase the population of the Sinai peninsula from one hundred thousand to two million over ten years by developing new farms, mines, and industries there.

Although the Arabs see Israel as the primary enemy, the

example of Israel is also the primary Arab goal. The Arab nations hope to accomplish the same economic miracles the Israelis proved were possible in desert lands. Arab advocates of compromise point out that as a Middle East partner, Israel could help bring about this transformation.

The hope for peace in the Middle East is brighter, ironically, precisely because the Arabs were not defeated in the Yom Kippur War. They no longer have to prove to themselves, the Israelis, or the world that they are courageous and inspirited fighters for their countries. Liberated from the feelings of humiliation and inferiority they have suffered since their defeats in 1948 and 1967, the Arab governments now feel free to turn their energies toward solving pressing domestic economic and social problems.

Their sense of pride and self-confidence has also been bolstered by OPEC's use of oil as a political weapon, compelling international respect, forcing the United States to pressure Israel into taking a more conciliatory attitude, and winning Palestinians the right to present their grievances before the nations of the world at the UN in January 1976.

These successes suggest that the Arabs will probably maintain their unity in OPEC over the sale, price, and handling of oil, but it is doubtful that they will be any more unified in other respects than they have been in the past. There is a possibility that they may split into two basic camps, with left-wing, socialist, and radical Arab nations on one side, and conservative, royalist, and right-wing Arab nations on the other.

There will also continue to be alliances of military expedience, cutting across the class struggle, such as that between Jordan and Syria in 1975 when they felt themselves threatened by Sadat's withdrawal from the anti-Israeli camp.

An unknown factor in the future of the Middle East must be the changes that can be expected from a new generation of

Arabs, who have already begun to outnumber their elders. In Egypt an incredible forty percent of the population today is younger than fifteen years old.

Arab youth sense that they belong to a generation that is likely to have the education, the opportunity, the power, and the will to remake their part of the world.

As they move further toward modernization, they also move away from the ancient, obsolete quarrels that kept the Arab nations divided and hostile over the centuries.

In their hands rests the new Arab tomorrow.

# Bibliography and Suggested Reading

Suggested further reading indicated by *

*Abu-Lughod, Ibrahim, ed. *The Arab-Israeli Confrontation of June 1967: An Arab Perspective*. Evanston: Northwestern University Press, 1970.

———.*Altered Realities: The Palestinians Since 1967*. North Dartmouth: Association of Arab-American University Graduates, Inc., 1973.

*Antonius, George. *The Arab Awakening*. New York: Capricorn Books, 1965.

Ashford, Douglas E. *Perspectives of a Moroccan Nationalist*. New Jersey: Bedminister Press, 1964.

*Aswad, Barbara C. *Arabic Speaking Communities in American Cities*. Staten Island: Center for Migration Studies of New York, Inc., 1974.

*Axelroth, Dorothy G., and Rabbi Leonard A. Schoolman. *Behind the Arab Mind*. New York: Union of American Hebrew Congregations, 1971.

Barlay, Stephen. *Bondage*. New York: Funk & Wagnalls, 1968.

*Berger, Morroe. *The Arab World Today*. New York: Doubleday, 1962.

Brinton, Jasper Yeates. *The Mixed Courts of Egypt*. New Haven: Yale University Press, 1968.

Bureau of Public Affairs. *Special Report: U.S. Policy in the Middle East*. Washington: State Department, 1974.

Burnett, Hugh, ed. *Face to Face*. New York: Stein and Day, 1965.

*Burton, Sir Richard. *The Arabian Nights Entertainments*. New York: The Heritage Press, 1955.

Canning, John. *100 Great Kings, Queens and Rulers of the World*. New York: Taplinger Publishing Company, 1967.

*Carmichael, Joel, and Alan Segal. *Arabs and Jews*. New York: Union of American Hebrew Congregations, 1969.

*Childers, Erskine B. *The Road to Suez*. London: McGibbon & Kee, 1962.

Committee on Internal Security, House of Representatives. *Terrorism*. Washington: U.S. Government Printing Office, 1974.

Cooley, John K. *East Wind Over Africa*. New York: Walker and Company, 1965.

Cremeans, Charles. *The Arabs and the World*. New York: Praeger, 1963.

*Duvignaud, Jean. *Change at Shebika*. New York: Pantheon, 1970.

Edwardes, Allen. *The Jewel in the Lotus*. New York: The Julian Press, Inc., 1959.

El Masry, Youssef. *Daughters of Sin*. New York: Macfadden, 1963.

*Elon, Amos. *The Israelis*. New York: Holt, Rinehart and Winston, 1971.

*Elton, Lord, ed. *General Gordon's Khartoum Journal*. New York: The Vanguard Press, Inc., undated.

*Elwan, Shwikar. *The Status of Women in the Arab World*. New York: The League of Arab States – Arab Information Center, 1974.

*Furlonge, Sir Geoffrey. *Palestine Is My Country*. New York: Praeger Publishers, 1969.

Gendzier, Irene. *A Middle East Reader*. New York: Penguin, 1969.

Gray, George Zabriskie. *The Children's Crusade*. New York: William Morrow & Company, Inc., 1972.

Gunther, John. *Inside Asia*. New York: Harper & Brothers, 1939.

———.*Procession*. New York: Harper & Row, 1965.

*Haddad, H. S. *Middle East History and the West*. North Dartmouth: Association of Arab-American University Graduates, Inc., 1973.

*Haslip, Joan. *The Sultan*. New York: Holt, Rinehart and Winston, 1958.

*Hegab, Sayed. *A New Egyptian*. New York: Praeger Publishers, 1971.

*Heikal, Mohammed Hassanein. *The Cairo Documents*. Garden City, N.Y.: Doubleday, 1973.

*Hitti, Philip K. *The Arabs*. Chicago: Regnery, 1970.

Hurwood, Bernhardt J. *Society and the Assassin*. New York: Parents' Magazine Press, 1970.

*Kalb, Marvin, and Bernard Kalb. *Kissinger*. Boston: Little, Brown and Company, 1974.

Keesing's Research Report. *The Arab-Israeli Conflict: The 1967 Campaign*. New York: Charles Scribner's Sons, 1968.

————. *Africa Independent*. New York: Charles Scribner's Sons, 1972.

Kenworthy, Leonard S., and Erma Ferrari. *Leaders of New Nations*. Garden City, N.Y.: Doubleday, 1968.

Kerr, Malcolm H. *The Arab Cold War: Gamal' Abd al-Nasir and His Rivals, 1958–1970*. London: Oxford University Press, 1971.

*Kimche, Jon. *The Second Arab Awakening*. London: Thames and Hudson, 1970.

*Kritzeck, James, ed. *Modern Islamic Literature*. New York: Holt, Rinehart and Winston, 1970.

Lacouture, Jean. *The Demigods*. New York: Alfred A. Knopf, 1970.

Lawrence, T. E. *Revolt in the Desert*. New York: George H. Doran Company, 1927.

Lewis, Bernard. *The Arabs in History*. New York: Harper & Row, 1966.

Lilienthal, Alfred. *What Price Israel?* Chicago: Regnery, 1953.

Lodge, Henry Cabot. *The Storm Has Many Eyes*. New York: W. W. Norton & Company, Inc., 1973.

Macdonald, R. W. *The League of Arab States*. Princeton, N.J.: Princeton University Press, 1965.

Magnus, Philip. *Kitchener*. London: Arrow Books, Ltd., 1961.

*Mallison, W. T., Jr. *The Balfour Declaration*. North Dartmouth: Association of Arab-American University Graduates, Inc., 1973.

*Mansfield, Peter. *The British in Egypt*. New York: Holt, Rinehart and Winston, 1971.

*McLeave, Hugh. *The Last Pharoah: Farouk of Egypt*. New York: The McCall Publishing Company, 1960.

*Mineau, Wayne. *The Go Devils*. London: Cassell, 1958.

Ministry of Oil and Minerals, Baghdad. *The Case of Raw-Materials Exporting Companies: Iraq's Viewpoint*. 1974.

Myers, Eugene A. *Arabic Thought and the Western World*. New York: Frederick Ungar Publishing Co., 1964.

*Nutting, Anthony. *The Arabs*. New York: New American Library, 1964.

Petran, Tabitha. *Syria*. New York: Praeger Publishers, 1972.

*Pfeiffer, Charles F. *The Arab-Israeli Struggle*. Grand Rapids, Mich.: Baker Book House, 1972.

Pilat, Oliver. *Drew Pearson*. New York: Harper's Magazine Press, 1973.

*Polk, William R. *The United States and the Arab World*. Cambridge, Mass.: Harvard University Press, 1975.

*Pryce-Jones, David. *The Face of Defeat: Palestinian Refugees and Guerrillas*. New York: Holt, Rinehart and Winston, 1972.

Quandt, William B. *The Politics of Palestinian Nationalism*. Santa Monica, Calif.: The Rand Corporation, 1971.

Rodinson, Maxime. *Israel and the Arabs*. New York: Pantheon, 1969.

*Ruedy, John, and Janet Abu-Lughod. *Dynamics of Land Alienation (in Palestine): The Demographic Transformation of Palestine*. North Dartmouth: Association of Arab-American University Graduates, Inc., 1973.

*St. John, Robert. *Israel*. New York: Time Incorporated, 1965.

*Schmidt, Dana Adams. *Armageddon in the Middle East*. New York: The John Day Company, 1974.

*Shahak, Israel. *The Shahak Report*. Washington, D. C.: Free Palestine, 1973.

Sharabi, Hisham. *Arab Intellectuals and the West*. Baltimore: The Johns Hopkins Press, 1970.

Sitwell, Sacheverell. *Mauretania*. London: Gerald Duckworth & Co., Ltd., 1951.

Smith, Wilfred Cantwell. *Islam in Modern History*. New York: The New American Library, 1957.

*Steegmuller, Francis. *Flaubert in Egypt*. Boston: Little, Brown and Company, 1972.

*Stephens, Robert. *Nasser: A Political Biography*. New York: Simon and Schuster, 1971.

*Stewart, Desmond. *The Arab World*. New York: Time Incorporated, 1964.

Terrasse, Henri. *History of Morocco*. Casablanca: Editions Atlantides, 1952.

Tolkunov, Leo. *The Middle East: From the Battlefield to the Negotiating Table*. Moscow: Novosti Press Agency Publishing House, 1974.

Toynbee, Arnold J. *East to West*. New York: Oxford University Press, 1958.

*Von Horn, Carl. *Soldiering for Peace*. New York: David McKay Company, Inc., 1967.

Yaffe, James. *The American Jews*. New York: Random House, 1968.

Yost, Charles. *The Conduct and Misconduct of Foreign Affairs*. New York: Random House, 1972.

Zagloul, Ahmed, and Zane Zagloul. *The Black Prince and Other Egyptian Folk Tales*. Garden City, N.Y.: Doubleday, 1971.

*Zionism: Instrument of Imperialist Reaction: Soviet Opinion on Events in the Middle East*. Moscow: Novosti Press Agency Publishing House, 1970.

*Zionist Israeli Acts of Terrorism: 1939–1974*. Washington, D.C.: Free Palestine, undated.

Also consulted were issues of the *Arab Economic Review*, the *Arab Report*, the *Atlanta Constitution*, the *Atlantic Monthly*, the *Center Magazine*, the *Detroit Free Press*, *Free China Weekly*, *Iraq News Bulletin*, *Lithopinion*, *Mankind*, *Middle East Forum*, *Moneysworth*, *Ms*, the *Nation*, *National Geographic*, *News from Saudi Arabia*, *Newsweek*, *New York*, *New York Post*, the *New York Times*.

In addition: materials obtained from the governments of Saudi Arabia, Iraq, Jordan, Lebanon, People's Democratic Republic of Yemen, Qatar, Morocco, the United States, the Soviet Union, the United Nations, and the League of Arab States.

# Index

Abbasids, 51, 52

Abdul-Hamid (Ottoman sultan), 66

Abdullah (Arabian prince), 67, 69, 70

Abdullah (Transjordan king), 93, 96, 99

Abdul Nasser, Gamal. *See* Nasser, Gamal Abdul

Abi-wardi (poet), 57

Abqaiq, Saudi Arabia, 160

Abu-Jaber, Kamel, 18

Abu Rudeis oil field, 139, 142

Aflaq, Michael, 84, 107

Ahmad, Jabir al, 174

Ahmad, Muhammad Sid, 182

Ahmed, Mohammed, 66

*Ahram, Al,* 182

air force, Israeli, 119, 120

airport massacres, 134, 139

Akins, James, 167

Alami, Musa, 84, 92, 93, 95

Alamut, Persia, 56

Al Fatah, 2, 5, 112, 132, 136; formation of, 106; fragmentation in, 7

Algeria, French control of, 66

Ali (son-in-law of Mohammed), 49

Ali, Mohammed (Turkish officer), 63

Allah, 14; *see also* Islam

Allenby, Edmund, 71, 72

Allon (Israeli foreign minister), 186

Alrashid, Rashid Abdulaziz, 158, 174

Amnesty International, 97

Amorites, 46

Anglo-Egyptian treaty, 86, 100

Anglo-Iranian Oil Company, 156, 159, 160

ANM. *See* Arab Nationalist Movement

anti-American demonstrations, 120

anti-British demonstrations, 120

anti-Semitism, 78, 146; accusations of, 146, 183

Arab, definition of, 22–23

Arab Empire: fall of, 58; Golden Age of, 52, 54; rise of, 22; spread of, 51

arabesque, 53

Arab Higher Committee, 93

Arab countries: and American-made products, 188; Arab support of, 177; have-not, 187; oil weapon of, 165 (*see also* Organization of Petroleum Exporting Countries); U.S. threats against, 166

Arabian-American Oil Company (ARAMCO), 156; American outposts of, 160; development by, 157; executives of, 18, 160–161; oil concession payments of, 158; profits of, 164; and social programs, 175; strikes against, 159

*Arabian Nights, The,* 52

Arabian Peninsula, warfare in, 83

Arab League, 43, 89, 90, 92, 109, 111, 117; Arab liberation army of, 93; defeat of, 95; economic boycott of, 98

Arab Legion, 136, 137

Arab Nationalist Movement (ANM), 133; *see also* nationalism

Arabs: attitudes of, 181 (*see also* values); Christian, 19, 29, 143; feuds among, 6; Israeli, 135; new generation of, 190–191; world opinion of, 1, 6, 11, 17; *see also* Bedouin

Arab syndrome, 171

Arab territory, Israel's occupation of, 18; *see also* land

Arab unity, concept of, 109, 111, 130; *see also* United Arab Republic

Arafat, Yasir, 5, 6, 15, 20, 94, 106; and Al Fatah, 112, 132; and King Hussein, 137; and PFLP, 136; and Sinai agreement, 145; as spokesman of Palestinian cause, 134; and Zionists, 183; *see also* Al Fatah

ARAMCO. *See* Arabian-American Oil Company

architecture, Arabic, 24, 52–53, 55

armistice, July 1949, 98

army: Arab liberation, 93; British Eighth, 89; Egyptian, 88, 113, 121; Egyptian Third, 140; Israeli, 120; of Jordan, 2

artisans, 60

arts, of Abassid empire, 52–53; *see also* architecture; literature

Assad, Hafiz al-, 117, 147

assassinations, 139

Assassins, 56

Assousa, George, 186

astronomy, 54

Aswan Dam, 40, 122; negotiations over, 102; Soviet support of, 149, 150

Athens Airport, PFLP attack on, 134

attitudes, Arab, 42; *see also* values

Awatmeh, Nayef, 133

Axelroth, Dorothy G., 180

Axis powers, 89; *see also* World War II

Ayesha (wife of Mohammed), 50

Azm, Khalid, 149

Azuri, Naguib, 81

Baath party, 32, 84, 107, 150
Babylonians, 46
Badr, battle of, 139
Badr, Mohammed el-, 109
Baghdad, Iraq, 51, 52, 58
Bahira (monk), 48
Bahrain, 168
Bakr, Abu, 50, 51
Balfour, Arthur, 70, 75
Balfour Declaration, 70, 71, 72, 73, 74, 81, 82, 87
Ball, George, 185
Bandung Conference, 100
Bank of the Commonwealth, Arab investment in, 169
Banna, Hassan al-, 83
Barzani, Mustafa, 32
baths, public, 59
Baybars, 58
Bedouin, 11, 24–27; in Jordan, 32, 96; and Lawrence of Arabia, 68; and oil companies, 158; and oil exploration, 157; religion of, 47; in Saudi Arabia, 30; strikes of, 159; "traditional," 19; Westernization of, 41–42; women of, 38
Beirut: American University of, 63; destruction of, 144; 1913 Arab congress in, 66
Beirut International Airport, Israeli raid against, 134
Bell, J. Bowyer, 124
Ben-Dak, Joseph, 184
Ben-Gurion, David, 81, 84–85, 94, 97, 105
Benjamin, R., 98
Berbers, 34, 35
Berger, Morroe, 15

Bernadotte, Folke, 94, 95
beys, and land reform, 101
birth control centers, Egyptian, 40, 101, 189
Bitar, Salah, 84, 107
blacklist, for Israeli supporters, 141
blackmail, energy, 165
Black September terrorist group, 2, 3, 4, 136, 138, 152
blockade, of Israeli shipping, 117–118
bombings: by Arab Higher Committee, 93; at Hebrew University, 135; by Israeli planes, 3, 131; letter, 2, 139; of Tel Aviv's Savoy Hotel, 144; at Zion Square, 6, 144
bonds, U.S., Arab purchase of, 169
Bourguiba, Habib, 34, 112
boycott: of Arab League, 98; Arab oil, 120, 167; OPEC, 162, 164; see also Organization of Petroleum Exporting Countries
Brezhnev, Leonid, 153
British Petroleum (BP), 160
British White Paper, on Jewish immigration, 90, 94
broadcasts, illegal, 87, 88
Bunche, Ralph, 95

Cairo, Egypt, 29, 58; Arab League in, 90; British in, 65; summit at, 111; women in, 189; see also Egypt
calligraphy, 53
camels, 25

cartel, oil, 156, 158; antitrust suit against, 160; profits of, 162; Western, 159; *see also* Organization of Petroleum Exporting Countries
casualties, of Six-Day War, 121
Cattan, Henry, 16, 181
cease-fire, UN, 121, 165
Central Intelligence Agency (CIA), in Iran, 160
Chamber of Commerce, United States–Arab, 170
Chamoun, Camille, 107
Charhadi, Driss Ben Hamed, 42
childbirth, 37, 38–39
children, socialization of, 37, 45; *see also* education
China: supports Israel, 183; and PLO radicals, 152
Chou En-lai, 121
Christians, Arab, 19, 29, 143
Church, Frank, 163–164
Churchill, Winston, 82
cities, Middle East, 28–29
clans, Bedouin, 25; *see also* Bedouin
"Coca-Cola-nization," 14
code of honor, 39; Bedouin, 26; *see also* values
Cold War, 100, 102, 149
colonialism, 61–76; *see also* France; Great Britain
commercial code, 64
Common Market, 183; Arab version of, 186, 187
communication, Arab-West, 10–11; *see also* public opinion
communism: international, 107; in Middle East, 136

Communist party: in Arab world, 154; Egyptian, 112
Comnenus, Alexius, 56
Compagnie Française, 156
conduct, rules of, 39; *see also* values
Congress, U.S., 145
*Congressional Quarterly,* 187
constitution, Egypt's, 102
cotton, Egyptian, 63, 65
counterterrorism, 5
crime, 43
Crusades, 56–60
culture, Moslem, 59; *see also* arts; religion; science; values

Daley, Richard, 146
Davignon, Etienne, 183
Dayan, Moshe, 121, 125, 126
Deir Yassin, massacre at, 93
de Lesseps, Ferdinand, 64
Delta Airlines, 169
democracy, Arab concept of, 12
détente, Soviet-American, 151
De Torres, Louis, 60
developing countries, and Saudi Arabia, 177; *see also* Third World
Dhahran, Saudi Arabia, 160
diaspora: Jewish, 77; Palestinian, 16, 78
Din, Nasir al-, 78
disease, 43
divorce, in Arab countries, 39; *see also* marriage
*djellaba,* wearing of, 40
Dome of the Rock, 14
Doughty, Charles, 27
drugstores, 55

du Camp, Maxime, 64
Dulles, John Foster, 102, 103, 107, 108, 149, 150
Duvignaud, Jean, 37, 39

East-West accord, 167
Eden, Anthony, 103
education: in Arab villages, 37; in Kuwait, 173–174; public, 40; in Saudi Arabia, 175
Egon, Nicholas, 169
Egypt: and Great Britain, 82, 86, 91, 100; public schools in, 12; sale of American military transport planes to, 188; sexual equality in, 40; Soviet military personnel in, 151; and USSR, 112; see also Nasser, Gamal Abdul; United Arab Republic
Egyptian Royal Military Academy, 86
Egyptian-Syrian alliance, 113, 115
Egyptians, 19, 31, 46
Eisenhower, Dwight D., 108, 160
Eisenhower Doctrine, 107
embargo, oil, 4–5, 8, 127, 163; see also boycott; cartel; oil; Organization of Petroleum Exporting Countries
"emergency decree on property of absentees," 98
Emergency Forces, UN, 116
emigration, Zionist, 72; see also immigration; settlement
emotionalism, 44; see also values
energy crisis, in Western world, 8; see also oil crisis; oil embargo
engineers, Egyptian, 43
England. See Great Britain
Eretz Israel, 90
Eshkol, Levi, 115
Europe: in Egypt, 62; Israeli support of, 183; see also France; Great Britain
Europeans, Arab view of, 54–55
expectations, unfulfilled, 43
Exxon, 156, 159, 160
Eyal, Eli, 186

Fahmy, Ismail, 153
Faisal (Saudi Arabian king), 83, 133, 140, 142, 176; assassination of, 6
Faisal (son of sherif of Mecca). See Feisal
family, Arab, 36–45; see also values
family planning clinics, in Egypt, 40, 101, 189
Faris, Nabih A., 15
farming, soilless, 174
Farouk (Egyptian king), 85, 89, 95, 99, 122
Fatah. See Al Fatah
fatalism, of Islam, 23; see also values
Fatima (daughter of Mohammed), 49
Fatimids, 55
Fedayeen, 1, 9, 97, 104, 131, 132; and Al Fatah, 133; captured, 138; Jordanian attacks on, 2; and Nasser, 129; raids, 34; and Sinai pact, 145

Feisal (son of sherif of Mecca), 68, 72, 73; Zionists and, 75, 78

fellahin (peasants), 27–28; and land reform, 101

feminist movement, in Middle East, 188–189; *see also* women

fifth column, Arabs as, 131

Flaubert, Gustave, 64

Ford, Gerald, 142, 145, 166, 187

Foundation for Arab-Israeli Reconciliation, 184, 187

France: and Arab world, 35, 42, 66, 70, 72; and Egypt, 62–63, 64–65, 103; and Syria, 84

Free Officers of Egypt, 88, 89, 99

Fuad, Ahmed, 82, 85

Fulbright, William, 108

Garrett, Stephen A., 138

Gaydos, Joseph, 170

Gaza Strip, 98; Israeli occupation of, 185; refugee flight to, 96

Genesis, 47

Genghis Khan, 58

geography, 53, 55

Germany, and oil crisis, 163

Ghali, Butros, 186

Gilmour, Ian, 125, 126

Golan Heights, 112, 146; fighting on, 121; Israeli claims to, 182; Israeli occupation of, 185

Gordon, Charles, 66

*Goumhouriya, Al,* 101

governments, Arab, 29, 44; Arab attitudes toward, 12

Great Britain: and Arab world, 71; betrayal of, 75; Egyptian interests of, 86, 100; and establishment of Palestine, 16–17; and oil crisis, 163; Palestinian rule of, 81; during Six-Day War, 120; and Suez Canal, 65

Green Shirts, 85

Grey, Edward, 82

Gruening, Ernest, 124

guerrilla warfare, 1938, 86; *see also* Fedayeen; terrorism

Gulf (oil company), 156, 160

Gulf of Aqaba, 105; blockade of, 117–118; after Six-Day War, 121

Gunther, John, 189

Habash, George, 133, 134, 135, 136

Haganah (Israeli defense force), 81, 90, 93, 94; British-trained members of, 87

Hamdan, Aharif al-, 172

Hamid, Abd al-, 65

Hamites, 46

Hammadi, Saadoun, 165

Hammarskjold, Dag, 107, 186

*Haolam Hazeh,* 147

harem, 40

Harkaby, Yehoshofat, 185

Harman, Abraham, 179–180

Harris poll, on Israeli conflict, 180

Harun. *See* Rashid, Harun al-

Hashemites, 82, 83

*Hawaa* (magazine), 189

Hebrew University, bombing at, 135

Hegira, 49; *see also* Mecca

Heikal, Mohammed Hassanein, 166, 170, 171
Hejaz, Saudi Arabia, 75
Henry, Krug, 157
Herzl, Theodore, 79
Herzog, Chaim, 179, 183
history: Arab, 45, 46–60; Biblical, 46; modern Arab, 61–76
Hitti, Philip K., 44, 47, 54
Hodgkins, C., 127
Hollings, Ernest, 166
Holmes, Frank, 40
holy war, 29, 49, 66, 93, 116
honor, code of, 26, 39
hospitality, Bedouin, 26; see also Bedouin; values
House of Knowledge, 53
Hout, Shafik, 7
Hussein (king of Jordan), 1, 2, 33, 99, 111, 118, 119; and Arafat, 137; and Fedayeen, 132, 133; and Nasser, 135, 178; and Palestinians, 136, 144; peace negotiations of, 128, 129; and Sadat, 143; UN address of, 126; and West Bank, 5; see also Jordan
hydroponics, 174

Ibn Abdel Aziz, Khalid, 142
Ibn Abdul Aziz, Fahed, 181
Ibn Abdul Wahab, Mohammed, 62
Ibn-al-Sabbah, Hassan, 56
Ibn Ali, Hussein, 67, 72, 75, 83
Ibn Khaldun (Arab scholar), 59, 62
Ibn Saud (Arabian king), 75, 83,

89, 91, 101, 110, 133; and oil exploration, 157
Ibn Saud, Mohammed, 62
Ibrahim (pasha of Egypt), 63
idolatry, 50
illiteracy, 175; British White Paper on, 87, 90, 94; UN on, 181
immigration, Jewish, 80, 81–82, 84, 85, 96, 182
independence, of Arab states, 75, 93; see also nationalism
Indonesia, in OPEC, 161
Indris (Libyan king), 135
industrialization, 189
inferiority, Arab feeling of, 96, 140, 190
infidels, 14, 29
inflation: Egyptian, 113; worldwide, 5, 165
Inquisition, 60
intellectuals, Palestinian, 181
International Court of Justice, 118
International Institute for Strategic Studies, 187
Iran: oil of, 159–160; in OPEC, 161; see also Anglo-Iranian Oil Company
Iraq: and Arab defense pact, 118; British control of oil in, 156; Communists in, 150; and oil exploration, 158; Soviet relations with, 152; in Yom Kippur War, 139
Iraq Petroleum Company, 156
Iraqis, 32
Irgun Zvai, 8, 84, 88, 90, 92, 93

Ishmaelites, 23
Islam: as city culture, 28–29; sects of, 29; and socialism, 21; teachings of, 13; *see also* Koran; religion
Ismael (Egypt's khedive), 65
Ismail, Moulay, 62
Israel: American support for, 179; Arab attitudes toward, 11, 14; establishment of, 15, 88–97; land disputes of, 80, 83, 96, 99; Palestinians in, 110; retaliation of, 3, 4, 147; Syrian border of, 113; U.S. military aid to, 163; *see also* Jews; Zionism
Israeli League for Human and Civil Rights, 18, 126
Italians, in Arab world, 66
Italy, and oil crisis, 163
*Izvestia,* 126, 182

Jackson, Henry, 165
Jahiliyah period, 48
Janissaries, 61
Japan, and oil crisis, 163
Jarring, Gunnar, 129
Jerusalem, 77; Arab evacuation of, 125; Arabs in, 132; after armistice of 1949, 98; Israeli annexation of, 123, 127
Jewish Agency, 83, 90, 92
Jewish National Home, 82
Jewry, Orthodox branch of, 180; *see also* Zionism
Jews, 46; and Arab culture, 15, 80; historical persecution of, 78; and Mohammed, 49; and relations with Arafat, 183

*jihad* (holy war), 29, 49, 66, 67, 68, 93, 116
*jizyah* (poll tax), 50
Job, 46–47
Jordan: and Arab defense pact, 118; Fedayeen in, 133; 1957 attempted coup in, 106; refugee flight to, 124; refugee population of, 96; in Yom Kippur War, 139; *see also* Transjordan
Judaea, 77
Judeo-Christian faith, message of, 48

Kanaan, Taher, 181
Karameh, battle of, 132
Kassem, Abdul Karim, 150
Kerr, Malcolm H., 8
Khadiji (wife of Mohammed), 48
Khalid (Saudi king), 143, 176
Khalidi, Usama, 16
Khan, Ayub, 189
Khartoum conference, 14, 127
Khashoggi, Adnan, 170
Khayyam, Omar, 54
Khittab, Hafiz, 85
Khrushchev, Nikita, 9, 116, 150
kibbutzim: and Arab land, 99; establishing, 84; raids against, 93; Syrian attacks on, 113; *see also* land; settlement
kidnappings, 139
Kinda (pre-Islamic kingdom), 47
King-Crane report, 73–74
Kissinger, Henry, 7, 9, 136, 145, 151, 153, 166, 167, 182, 185; shuttle diplomacy of, 140, 142, 153

Kitchener, Herbert, 66
Knesset, 184
Koran, 13, 23, 24, 26, 48, 51, 178; on women, 36; *see also* Islam
Koraysh (tribe), 48, 49
Kuanhua, Chiao, 183
Kuwait: oil deposits in, 157–158; oil embargo of, 161; and oil exploration, 158; social programs in, 172–174; wealth of, 168; women in, 40–41
Kuwaitis, 31; investments in U.S., 169

Labor party, Israeli, 183
land, Jewish-Arab dispute over, 80, 83, 96, 99; *see also* kibbutzim
land reform, Egyptian, 101, 122
language: of ancient Arabs, 47; Arabic, 45, 51, 55, 69; religion and, 44
"lawful magic," 44
Lawrence, Thomas Edward (Lawrence of Arabia), 23, 68, 72, 73
*Lawrence of Arabia,* 69
Lebanese, 33
Lebanon: civil war in, 143, 144, 147; establishment of, 75; Fedayeen in, 133; Israeli attacks on, 147; pro-Nasser rebels in, 107; refugee flight to, 124; Soviet relations with, 152
League of Nations, 83
letter bombs, 2, 139
libraries, of Arab world, 54
Libya: coup in, 135; Soviet support of, 153; wealth of, 168
literacy, rising rate of, 188
literature, Arabian, 5; oral, 26–27, 44, 47
lobby: oil, 158, 160; Zionist, 120
Lockheed Aircraft, 169
Lodge, Henry Cabot, 108

Mahdi, the, 66
Majali, Abdel Wahab, 127
Maksoud, Clovis, 179
Mamalukes, 55, 63
Mamun. *See* Rashid, Mamun al-
Mansfield, Mike, 186
Mao Tse-tung, 121
Marie-Therese, Sister, 125
marines, in Lebanon, 107
marriage, in Arab world, 38–39; *see also* family; women
Marsalha, Ahmen, 135
Marxists, 120
Masudi (geographer), 55
mathematics, Arab, 54
Mayhew, Christopher, 119
McGovern, George, 181
McMahon, Henry, 67
McMahon-Hussein accord, 70
Mecca, Saudi Arabia, 30, 48, 83
medicine, Arabic, 55
Medina, Saudi Arabia, 30; flight to, 49
Middle East: American businessmen in, 170–171; peace in, 190; *see also individual countries*
*misbaha* beads, 33
Mixed Armistice Commission (MAC), 107, 118
Mobil, 156, 160

modernization, 189, 191

Mohammed, 14, 48–50; *see also* Islam

Mongols, 58, 59

monotheism, 47

Morocco, 35, 62; as French protectorate, 66

Morton, Rogers C. B., 166

Moses, 46

Moslem Brotherhood, 83, 85, 88, 93, 100

Moslems, population of, 13

Mossadegh, Mohammed, 159, 160

movies, effect of, 188

Moyne, Lord, 90

Moynihan, Daniel Patrick, 146

Mufti of Jerusalem, 84, 86, 88, 90, 93

multinational corporations: Senate subcommittee on, 164; in Suez Canal zone, 141

Munich, terrorism at Olympics, 3, 7, 139

music, 59

Napoleon, in Egypt, 62–63

Nasr, Seyyed Hossain, 55

Nasser, Gamal Abdul, 9, 13, 18, 28, 86, 94, 95, 99; and Anglo-Egyptian treaty, 100; and Bourguiba, 112; and Cold War, 100, 102, 149; and Communist world, 108; death of, 137; leadership of, 105–106; on Libyan coup, 135; plots against, 103, 104; prestige of, 114; and Resolution 242, 129; Soviet Union and, 149; tendered resignation of, 122; and UAR, 107; and U.S., 149; in Western press, 123; and Yemen republic, 110

nationalism, Arab, 76, 81, 107, 122, 137, 185

navigation, 59

Nazer, Isham, 176

Nazis, German, 78, 84, 91

NBC poll, on Israeli support, 180

*New York Times*, 117; Zionist influence on, 169

Nicholson, Harold, 70

1948 War, 94–96, 117

Nixon, Richard M., 136, 170

Nordau, Max, 79

North Yemen, Soviet relations with, 153; *see also* Yemen

Nutting, Anthony, 26, 128

oil: nationalization of, 162; U.S. dependency on, 155; as weapon, 163, 166

oil companies, 164, 166; price increases of, 165; *see also* cartel, oil

oil-consuming nations, 167

oil crisis, 164

oil embargo, 4–5, 163; consequences of, 8; of 1967, 127

oil lobby, 158, 160

oil tax, U.S., 159

"Old Man of the Mountains," 56

Olympics, murders at Munich, 3, 7, 139

Oman: People's Front for Liberation in, 20; wealth of, 168

Omar (Islamic caliph), 51
OPEC. *See* Organization of Petroleum Exporting Countries
opinion, world, 1, 6, 7, 11, 17
Organization of Petroleum Exporting Countries (OPEC), 5, 161; and Arab pride, 190; Kissinger threat to, 9; prices, 167; attack on Vienna headquarters of, 147; Western attitudes toward, 8; Western business partners of, 163
Osman, Osman Ahmed, 189
Oteifi, Gamel el-, 182
Ottoman Empire, 60, 61; and Europe, 66, 68; overthrow of, 67; surrender of, 72
overpopulation, 43, 101; in Egypt, 177–178

Palestine: Arab claims to, 77; establishment of, 75; partitioning of, 91; rule of, 78
Palestine Liberation Organization (PLO), 2, 111, 112, 117, 147; and Egypt, 7; guerrilla forces of, 143; spokesmen of, 14–15; terrorist campaign of, 6
Palestine Mixed Armistice Commission, 107, 118
Palestine National Council, 133
Palestinian refugees, 14; despair of, 9; Israeli treatment of, 125–126, 128; plight of, 15; and UNRWA, 106; *see also* refugee camps
Palestinians: changing Israeli attitudes toward, 184; displaced,
18; in Israel, 110, 125; on Israeli-occupied West Bank, 137–138; Israeli treatment of, 126; numbers of, 33–34; settlement with, 185; sympathy with, 181; and USSR, 152
parliament, Egyptian, 65
partition: of Palestine, 92; of Syria, 75
Pasha, Arabi, 65
Pasha, Jemal, 67, 68, 71
Pasha, Nahas, 89
peace agreement, interim, 185; *see also* Sinai agreement
peace talks, and Palestinians, 5
peaceful coexistence, 186
peasants, Arab, 27–28; changing lives of, 188; *see also* fellahin
Peel Commission, 86
Persia, oil strike in, 156
Persians, influence of, 51–52
petrodollars, 168
Pfeiffer, Charles F., 184
PFLP. *See* Popular Front for the Liberation of Palestine
Phalangist party, 6, 143
Pharaon, Ghaith, 169
pharmacies, 55
Philip III (Spanish king), 62
Phoenicians, 46
Picot, F. Georges, 67
plague, 55
PLO. *See* Palestine Liberation Organization
poets, Arabic, 52, 57, 117
Poitiers, Battle of, 51
poll tax, 50

Polo, Marco, 56
polygamy, 38
Popular Democratic Front for the Liberation of Palestine (PDFLP), 133
Popular Front for the Liberation of Palestine (PFLP), 1, 2, 133, 134, 138; documentary film of, 20; skyjackings of, 137; terrorism by, 136
postal service, 59
poverty, 43
prejudice, anti-Arab, 8, 11; *see also* public opinion
press: American, 169; Western, 11, 123
prices, oil, 156, 162; *see also* oil companies
propaganda, Nasser's, 124
Pryce-Jones, David, 20, 138
public opinion: and Arab leaders, 179–180; U.S., 9; Western, 9; world, 1, 6, 7, 11, 17
public schools, in Egypt, 12; *see also* education
punishment, 43–44

Qaddafi, Muammar al-, 30, 135, 144; and oil cartel, 162; Soviet support of, 153
Qatar: social programs in, 177; wealth of, 168
Quandt, William, 180

Rabbinical Council of America, 180
Rabin, Itzhak, 113, 115, 141, 181, 183
Radio Cairo, 120

raids, of Al Fatah, 112
Rajab, Muhammad, 184
Ramani, Sheikh, 162
Rashid, Harun al- (Abbasid caliph), 52, 53
Rashid, Mamun al- (Abbasid caliph), 53, 54, 55
Rashid, Mohammed, 7, 16
Ras Tanura, Saudi Arabia, 160
*rawis* (storytellers), 45
Recitation, 48; *see also* Koran
Red Cross, 94, 96
refugee camps: Palestinian, 121; in Gaza Strip, 96; Israeli attacks on, 3; during Six-Day War, 120; standard of living in, 138
refugees. *See* Palestinian refugees
religion: in Arab life, 19, 23; in Kuwait, 173, 174; language and, 44; Moslem, 23; *see also* Islam
Resolution 242, of UN Security Council, 4, 128, 129, 163
Resolution 338, UN Security Council, 152
*Revolt in the Desert,* 68
rhetoric, Arab, 9; *see also* language
Richard the Lion Hearted, 57
Rida, Rashid, 44
Riyadh, Saudi Arabia, girls' college in, 176
Rommel, Erwin, 89
Roosevelt, Franklin D., 89, 91
Rothschild, Lord, 73, 78, 79
Royal Dutch–Shell, 156, 159
*Rubaiyat,* 54

Sabah, Sheikh (Kuwait's foreign minister), 166
Sadat, Anwar, 7, 86, 88, 99, 137, 139, 140, 141, 143; foreign policy of, 190; plots against, 144; in U.S., 146; and withdrawal of Soviet military personnel, 151–152
Said, Edward, 17
Said, Amina el-, 189
Saladin, 57–58
Saliba, Jamil, 42
Salim, Sabah al-, 31, 172
Sammu, attack on, 113
Samuel, Herbert, 76, 81
San Remo Conference, 75, 76
Sarid, Joseph, 184, 186
Sarraj, Abdul Hamid, 106
Saud dynasty, 157
Saudi Arabia: antistrike laws of, 159; Bedouin in, 27 (*see also* Bedouin); establishment of, 83; oil embargo of, 161; search for oil in, 157; social programs in, 172, 175–177; wealth of, 168; women in, 41
schism, in Islam, 51
Schlesinger, James, 166
Schmidt, Dana Adams, 92, 106
scholars, Arab, 54, 60, 63
Schonfeld, Fabian, 180
Schoolman, Leonard A., 180
science, 59, 60; astronomy, 54; geography, 53, 55; mathematics, 54; medicine, 55
sectarianism, in Syria, 31
Security Council, UN, 5; Resolution 242 of, 4, 128, 129, 163; Resolution 338 of, 152

Selim I (Ottoman sultan), 60
Sem (tribe), 46
"Semite," 46
Septembrists, 2, 3, 4, 136, 138, 152
settlement: Jewish, 84; Zionist, 80, 81; *see also* kibbutzim; land
Seven Sisters, 160, 161
Shahak, Israel, 18, 126
Shahak Report, 126
Shalesh, Jamil, 32
Shalmaneser III (Assyrian king), 47
Sharon, Ariel, 182
Shaw Commission, British, 83
*Sheik of Araby,* 69
sheikhs, 25
Shell (British-Dutch oil company), 160
Shia sect, 19, 29, 51
Shukairy, Ahmed, 14–15, 111, 117
"shuttle diplomacy," 140, 142, 153
Simon, William E., 166
Sinai: Israeli claims to, 182; oil in, 123; population in, 189
Sinai agreement, 186; interim, 145
Sinbad the Sailor, 52
Sivan, Emanuel, 184
Six-Day War, 115–130; Arab defeat in, 11; and oil embargo, 161; and Soviet-American relations, 151; start of, 119
Skina, Ansbert G., 170
skyjackings, 1, 2, 137
Smith, Wilfred Cantwell, 45

Socal (oil company), 160
social change, in Middle East, 188
socialism: Egyptian, 101, 109; in Middle East, 21
social reforms, Nasser's, 113
Society of Free Officers, 99; *see also* Free Officers of Egypt
South Carolina, Arab investment in, 169
Soviet Union: Arab relations with, 148; Egyptian relations with, 102, 141; Palestinian support of, 182; during Six-Day War, 120
Spain, Moslem influence on, 55
special forces, U.S., 167
"Special Night Squads," 87
Srour, Heiny, 20, 41
standard of living: Arab, 43, 178; Egyptian, 101; in Kuwait, 172
Standard Oil of California, 156, 161
Stephen of Cloyes, 58
Stern, Abraham, 88
Stern gangs, 8, 88, 90, 93, 95
storytellers, 45; *see also* literature; poets
Sudan, 66
Suez Canal, 64–65, 86, 97, 120; nationalizing of, 103; reopening of, 142–144
Suez War, 104–105
Sufi movement, 59
Suleiman, Michael W., 17
Sultan, Najat al-, 41
sultans, Ottoman, 61
Sumerians, 46

Sunnis, 19, 29, 59
Sykes, Mark, 67, 72
Sykes-Picot accord, 67, 71, 74
Syria: and Lebanese civil war, 147; oil workers in, 159; partitioning of, 75; PLO support of, 144; refugee flight to, 96, 124; relations with Egypt, 112; relations with U.S., 150; sectarianism in, 31, 32; Sinai pact and, 146; after Six-Day War, 123; and Soviet Union, 107, 149, 152, 153; in UAR, 109; women in, 41
Syrians, 19, 31

taboos, Islamic, 24
Tal, Wesfi, assassination of, 2
Taleb, Abu, 48
Tamerlane, 60
Tamraz, Roger, 169
tankers, oil, 159
Tariki, Abdulla, 18
Tartars, 60
technicians: American, 186; American, in Sinai buffer zone, 142; Russian, 151
technology, in Arab world, 123
television, in Arab villages, 188
Tenth Zionist Congress, 81
terrorism: Arab, 2–4, 5, 86; Irgun, 8, 84, 87, 88, 90, 92, 93; Israeli, 2–4, 5, 90; Mideast, 18; Septembrists, 2, 3, 4, 136, 138, 152; Stern gangs, 8, 88, 90, 93, 95; Zionist, 92
Tewfik (Egypt's khedive), 65
Texaco, 156, 160

Thabet, Reda, 169
Thant, U., 116
Third World: and Nasser, 100; and OPEC cartel, 177; and Palestinians, 146
Tiberias, battle at, 57
*Time* magazine, 126
Titus, 77
Tokunov, Lev, 182
torture, 138
Toynbee, Arnold, 15, 105
tradition: desert, 27; oral, 44
Transjordan: establishment of, 82; refugee flight to, 96; *see also* Jordan
tribes: Berbers, 34, 35; Bedouin, 25 (*see also* Bedouin); Koraysh, 48; Omayyad, 49; Sem, 46
truce, UN, 97
Truce Supervisory Organization, UN, 107
true believers, 14
Truman, Harry S., 91
Tunisia, French control of, 66
Tunisians, 34
Turkish empire, 55; *see also* Ottoman Empire
Turks, and Arab world, 67

UAR. *See* United Arab Republic
Umayyads, 51, 56
unemployment, 43; *see also* education
unification, pan-Arab, 30, 109, 111, 130
Union of American Hebrew Congregations, 180

United Arab Emirates, wealth of, 168
United Arab Republic (UAR): formation of, 107; Syria in, 150; Syrian withdrawal from, 109
United Nations: condemnation of Israel, 113; Expeditionary Force of (UNEF), 105; and 1948 War, 94; on Palestine, 91; Relief and Works Agency (UNRWA), 3, 34, 95, 106; Truce Supervisory Organization of, 107
United States: and Arab boycott, 98; Arab investment in, 169–170; Egyptian relations with, 141; foreign policy of, 180; oil lobby of, 158, 160, 162; during Six-Day War, 120; threats of, 166
"unity of purpose," 101–102
"unity of ranks," 102
universities, Syrian, 41
UNRWA. *See* United Nations, Relief and Works Agency
urbanization, in deserts, 175

Valentino, Rudolph, 69
values, Arabic, 69; Bedouin, 26–27; family, 36–45; honor, 26, 39; individualism, 42; Kuwaiti, 174; *see also* Islam; religion
veil, wearing of, 40
Venezuela, in OPEC, 161
Versailles Peace Conference, 72, 73, 74

Vikings, Arab view of, 54
villages, Arab, 28; attacks on, 97;
    families of, 37; radio in, 188;
    *see also* kibbutzim; settlement
Voice of Israel, 87
von Horn, Carl, 107

Wahabis, 62, 63, 83
Wailing Wall, 83
Walters, Dennis, 125, 126
Ward, Shirley, 164
Wasfi Tal. *See* Tal, Wasfi
Weizmann, Chaim, 59, 71, 72,
    73, 84
West, influence on Arab world,
    38, 41, 59, 64
West Bank, 96, 98, 147; Arab
    evacuation of, 125; state of
    Palestine on, 181, 186; Israeli
    claims to, 182; Israeli capture
    of, 121, 123; occupation of,
    137–138, 185
West Bank activists, 20
White Paper, British, 90, 94
Wilson, Woodrow, 70, 71, 73
women, Arab, 35; in Arab Em-
    pire, 52; attitudes toward, 37;
    Bedouin, 26, 36, 38; in Cairo,
    189; Egyptian, 40; in marriage,
    39; in modern Arab world,
    61–62; in Saudi Arabia, 175–
    176
women's liberation movement, in
    Arab world, 40, 174

World War I, Arab world during,
    86
World War II, 87, 158; Arab
    states during, 89–90

Yaffi, Abdulla, 133
Yamani, Zaki, 161
Yariv, Aharon, 147
Yassin, Hassan, 38
Year of Calamity, 76
Year of Flight, 49
Yemen: civil war in, 118; revolu-
    tion in, 109; war in, 113, 127;
    *see also* North Yemen
Yom Kippur War, 4, 19, 139,
    190; end of, 5; significance of,
    140; Soviet supplies for, 152;
    U.S. supply for, 152
Yost, Charles, 119
youth, Arab, 191

Zangwill, Israel, 79
Zayyat, Mohammed H. al-, 128
Zionism, 8, 15; Arab fear of, 149,
    169; Arafat's view of, 183; ar-
    guments of, 16; birth of, 79;
    claims of, 77; Great Powers'
    commitment to, 74; and immi-
    gration to Palestine, 69, 71,
    72–73, 81; and Nazi Germany,
    84; during World War II, 87,
    90
Zionist Program, 74
Zion Square, bombing at, 6, 144